AUTO HOME LIFE

A Century of Service

1907 - 2007

A Century of Service
1907 – 2007

Jeffrey L. Rodengen

Edited by Elizabeth Fernandez and Jill Gambill
Design and layout by Sandy Cruz and Elijah Meyer

Write Stuff Enterprises, Inc.
1001 South Andrews Avenue
Fort Lauderdale, FL 33316
1-800-900-Book (1-800-900-2665)
(954) 462-6657
www.writestuffbooks.com

Copyright © 2007 by Write Stuff Enterprises, Inc. All rights reserved. No part of this book may be reproduced or transmitted in any form by any means, electronic or mechanical, including photocopying and recording, or by any information storage or retrieval system, without permission in writing from the publisher.

The publisher has made every effort to identify and locate the source of the photographs included in the edition of *Amica: A Century of Service*. Grateful acknowledgement is made to those who have kindly granted permission for the use of their materials in this edition. If there are instances where proper credit was not given, the publisher will gladly make any necessary corrections in subsequent printings.

Publisher's Cataloging in Publication
(Prepared by The Donohue Group, Inc.)

Rodengen, Jeffrey L.
   Amica : a century of service, 1907-2007 / Jeffrey L. Rodengen ; edited by Elizabeth Fernandez and Jill Gambill ; design and layout by Sandy Cruz and Elijah Meyer.

   p. ; cm.

   Includes index.
   ISBN-13: 978-1-932022-14-8
   ISBN-10: 1-932022-14-7

1. Automobile Mutual Insurance Company of America—History. 2. Insurance companies—United States—History. 3. Insurance, Automobile—United States—History. I. Fernandez, Elizabeth. II. Gambill, Jill. III. Cruz, Sandy. IV. Meyer, Elijah. V. Title. VI. Title: Century of service, 1907-2007

HG8540.A433 R63 2007   368.006/5
                                 2005935468

Library of Congress
Catalog Card Number: 2005935468

Completely produced in the
United States of America
10 9 8 7 6 5 4 3 2 1

Also by Jeffrey L. Rodengen

The Legend of Chris-Craft

IRON FIST:
The Lives of Carl Kiekhaefer

Evinrude-Johnson and
The Legend of OMC

Serving the Silent Service:
The Legend of Electric Boat

The Legend of Dr Pepper/Seven-Up

The Legend of Honeywell

The Legend of Briggs & Stratton

The Legend of Ingersoll-Rand

The Legend of Stanley:
150 Years of The Stanley Works

The MicroAge Way

The Legend of Halliburton

The Legend of York International

The Legend of Nucor Corporation

The Legend of Goodyear:
The First 100 Years

The Legend of AMP

The Legend of Cessna

The Legend of VF Corporation

The Spirit of AMD

The Legend of Rowan

New Horizons:
The Story of Ashland Inc.

The History of American Standard

The Legend of Mercury Marine

The Legend of Federal-Mogul

Against the Odds:
Inter-Tel—The First 30 Years

The Legend of Pfizer

State of the Heart: The Practical Guide
to Your Heart and Heart Surgery
with Larry W. Stephenson, M.D.

The Legend of Worthington Industries

The Legend of IBP

The Legend of Trinity Industries, Inc.

The Legend of
Cornelius Vanderbilt Whitney

The Legend of Amdahl

The Legend of Litton Industries

The Legend of Gulfstream

The Legend of Bertram
with David A. Patten

The Legend of Ritchie Bros. Auctioneers

The Legend of ALLTEL
with David A. Patten

The Yes, you can of Invacare Corporation
with Anthony L. Wall

The Ship in the Balloon:
The Story of Boston Scientific and the
Development of Less-Invasive Medicine

The Legend of Day & Zimmermann

The Legend of Noble Drilling

Fifty Years of Innovation: Kulicke & Soffa

Biomet—From Warsaw to the World
with Richard F. Hubbard

NRA: An American Legend

The Heritage and Values of RPM, Inc.

The Marmon Group: The First Fifty Years

The Legend of Grainger

The Legend of The Titan Corporation
with Richard F. Hubbard

The Legend of Discount Tire Co.
with Richard F. Hubbard

The Legend of Polaris
with Richard F. Hubbard

The Legend of La-Z-Boy
with Richard F. Hubbard

The Legend of McCarthy
with Richard F. Hubbard

Intervoice: Twenty Years of Innovation
with Richard F. Hubbard

Jefferson-Pilot Financial:
A Century of Excellence
with Richard F. Hubbard

The Legend of HCA

The Legend of Werner Enterprises
with Richard F. Hubbard

The History of J. F. Shea Co.
with Richard F. Hubbard

True to Our Vision
with Richard F. Hubbard

The Legend of Albert Trostel & Sons
with Richard F. Hubbard

The Legend of Sovereign Bancorp
with Richard F. Hubbard

Innovation is the Best Medicine:
The extraordinary story of Datascope
with Richard F. Hubbard

The Legend of Guardian Industries

The Legend of
Universal Forest Products

Changing the World: Polytechnic
University—The First 150 Years

Nothing is Impossible: The Legend
of Joe Hardy and 84 Lumber

In it for the Long Haul:
The Story of CRST

The Story of Parsons Corporation

Cerner: From Vision to Value

New Horizons:
The Story of Federated Investors

Office Depot: Taking Care of Business—
The First 20 Years

The Legend of General Parts:
Proudly Serving a World in Motion

Bard: Power of the Past,
Force of the Future

TABLE OF CONTENTS

Introduction vi

Acknowledgments viii

Chapter I   One Small Room 10

Chapter II   A Beaten Path to Our Door 20

Chapter III   From Coast to Coast 34

Chapter IV   Dynamic Growth 46

Chapter V   Dynamic Challenges, Consistent Growth 58

Chapter VI   In Unity, Growth 72

Chapter VII   Just the Best 86

Chapter VIII   Into the Modern Era 106

Notes to Sources 132

Index 138

Introduction

IN 1907, AMERICA WAS ON the verge of great change. The United States then consisted primarily of farms and small towns, while horses and coal-fed locomotives remained the chief modes of transportation, despite the invention of the automobile.

Adolph Thomas Vigneron, however, anticipated that automobiles would soon play a larger role in the country's future. In one small room, he founded the Automobile Mutual Insurance Company of America (Amica) in Providence, Rhode Island. Vigneron, an inventor and businessman, envisioned Amica as a mutual company, owned by policyholders instead of stockholders. He introduced the concept of preferred risk underwriting to the nascent field of car insurance, forgoing "soliciting agents" to rely exclusively on personal referrals from existing policyholders instead. Vigneron also understood the importance of making exceptional customer service the core of Amica's business philosophy.

During World War II, Amica served as a fiduciary agent of the War Damage Corporation, insuring the homes of policyholders against damage from enemy combatants. Still, roughly 98 percent of Amica's business came from automobile insurance. Amica persevered, despite a scarcity of manufacturing materials that forced car companies to halt production of new models. Amica also had half of its male employees and several female employees called into service for their country, yet the company refused to request a single employee military service deferment. Instead, Amica's remaining employees worked diligently to ensure the company's commitment to its customers remained strong.

Starting in 1962, *Consumer Reports* began a long-standing tradition of bestowing its top ratings on Amica, thanks in part to Amica's unusually high ratio of employees to policyholders, and its policy of paying underwriters a salary instead of commission. Since then, Amica has received the No. 1 score for automobile and homeowners insurance companies in *Consumer Reports* surveys on 18 different occasions. As an additional honor, Amica received its 12th and 13th J.D. Power awards in 2006, receiving the rank of "Highest Customer Satisfaction Among National Auto Insurers" for the seventh consecutive year and "Highest Customer Satisfaction Among National Homeowner Insurers" for the fifth year in a row.

Much of Amica's success stems from the dedication of its employees. From employing two clerks in 1907, Amica has grown to include a staff of more than 3,000 associates countrywide, with an average tenure of more than a decade. Amica's workforce has contributed to a corporate culture frequently referred to as the "Amica Family." This philosophy has helped the company maintain its unfaltering commitment to integrity and customer service as it has expanded to include services such as home, condominium, and renters insurance, as well as life insurance and personal umbrella liability coverage.

Amica's firm business principles have helped the business thrive through the years. Although Amica has never strived to be the biggest insurance company in the country, it prides itself on being the best. With branches across the country, the company continues to provide outstanding customer service to its policyholders and always pays claims promptly and fairly.

Amica's President and CEO Robert DiMuccio believes that it is the company's commitment to the traditional values of service, ethics, and loyalty that have set it apart. These values remain key to Amica's success, as DiMuccio explained:

I feel a sacred trust. [Amica] is a special place. … The company is in its 100th year, and I want to make sure that we move the company forward and get ready for its next 100 years. I truly hope there is somebody sitting in this seat 100 years from now. The company will look very different, I would suspect. It will adopt the technology and methods of the time period, but I hope the ethics are still here. Now that is what I see as my goal—to propel Amica into its next century of existence.

Acknowledgments

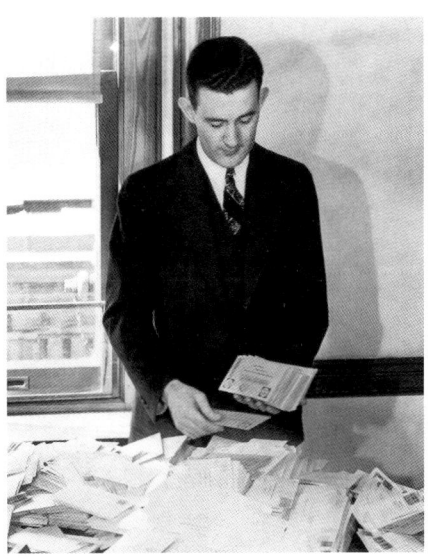

RESEARCHING, WRITING, AND PUBLISHING *Amica: A Century of Service 1907–2007* would have been impossible without the help of many individuals.

The development of the historical timelines and a large portion of the principal archival research was accomplished by research assistant Thomas Lowenstein. His thoughtful and careful work made it possible to publish a great deal of new information about the origins of Amica.

Elizabeth Fernandez and Jill Gambill, senior editors, organized the text and photos, while the artistic efforts of Sandy Cruz, vice president/creative director, and Elijah Meyer, graphic designer, brought the story to life.

Special thanks are due to Amica's corporate communications department as well as all Amica employees, past and present, who enriched this book by discussing their experiences.

Finally, special thanks are extended to the dedicated staff at Write Stuff Enterprises, Inc.: Stanimira Stefanova, executive editor; Ann Gossy and Heather Lewin, senior editors; Ryan Milewicz, graphic designer; Roy Adelman, on-press supervisor; Lynn C. Jones, proofreader; Mary Aaron, transcriptionist; Christine Michaud, indexer; Amy Major, executive assistant to Jeffrey L. Rodengen; Marianne Roberts, executive vice president, publisher, and chief financial officer; Steven Stahl, director of marketing; and Sherry Pawlirzyn–Hasso, bookkeeper.

The tall, light-colored building on the left, 10 Weybosset Street, known as "the skyscraper" of Providence, was the original home of Amica.

CHAPTER ONE

ONE SMALL ROOM
1907–1920

From the very beginning, Amica's emphasis on fair claim coverage and fast service guided the company through a century of unprecedented change to where it is today—a $3 billion company widely respected as one of the best insurance companies in the country.

IN 1907, AMERICA WAS PRIMARILY a country of small towns and rural living, where the main mode of transportation was still the horse-drawn carriage. While the nation boasted an energetic and rapidly expanding population of 85 million, there were still only 25,000 automobiles on the roads. Automobiles were rare enough that many Americans agreed with future President Woodrow Wilson, who called the new mode of transportation "a picture of arrogance of wealth, with all its independence and carelessness."[1] Taking a ride in an auto involved wearing a heavy coat, or "duster," and goggles or a veil.

However, America was on the verge of great change. Already, vast stretches of the world were becoming increasingly connected under the influence of the wireless telegraph and steamships, which could cross the Atlantic in only a little more than five days. In Detroit, Henry Ford announced his intention to create "a motor car for the great multitude" and set out to revolutionize not only transportation, but the way Americans lived.[2]

In 1898, only 200 autos were manufactured in the United States.[3] While the 25,000 in use nine years later might not seem abundant by modern standards, the trend was set for rapid growth in the automobile industry.

Ford was not the only American businessman who understood that the automobile was an inevitable part of the country's future. In Providence, Rhode Island, in the spring of 1907, Adolph Thomas Vigneron of the What Cheer Mutual Fire Insurance Company saw the changes automobiles brought to American life and had an idea.

Envisioning that the automobile would become increasingly important to how Americans lived, he set out to create a company that would apply the principle of "preferred risk" insurance to automobiles. "Mr. A. T.," as he was affectionately known by his close associates, brought together a group of prominent local businessmen to create the Automobile Mutual Insurance Company of America (Amica), endowing it from the very beginning with a philosophy of fair claim coverage and fast service.

10 Weybosset Street

Vigneron had a superior intellect and an inventive nature. He had come up with improvements to the typewriter carriage and held a patent for the

---

Adolph T. Vigneron, founder of the Automobile Mutual Insurance Company of America (Amica). Vigneron created Amica when he envisioned that the automobile would become increasingly important to how Americans lived. *(Photo by Fabian Bachrach.)*

development of a wool-spinning machine. He traveled widely in Europe and America, despite a handicap from infancy that made it impossible for him to walk without the aid of a heavy leg brace and a cane. His abundant energy and friendly nature made him a natural leader.[4]

In late 1906 and early 1907, Vigneron had the foresight to combine two existing concepts in the insurance industry and apply them for the first time to automobile insurance. The first concept was that the new company should only take on clients with strong character, prudent judgment, and responsible behavior, because these factors were the clearest indicators of the degree of risk involved in a given policy. This concept, known as "preferred risk underwriting," had existed in the world of fire insurance for close to 100 years, because no company wanted to insure a building that was insufficiently protected against fire. Vigneron saw that the most important aspect of risk assessment was understanding the people who were being insured. Prudent, cautious people would be less risky to insure, so these were the people the new insurance company sought to insure.[5] The company would do without soliciting agents, relying solely on personal referrals from existing policyholders.

Additionally, Vigneron decided that the new company would be a mutual company, owned by its policyholders instead of outside stockholders. In this way, each policyholder would be responsible for the success of the company as a whole and would therefore only recommend other cautious, prudent people to the company. Furthermore, on the anniversary date of each policy, the policyholders would receive a dividend from the company—a percentage of their original premium based on the profit of the company during the policy year. These dividends would lower the overall cost of insurance for each policyholder, providing an incentive for pol-

A circus parade passes through downtown Providence, circa 1910.

icyholders to recommend only desirable, low-risk acquaintances to Amica for insurance.

Vigneron also realized from the beginning that the best measure of an insurance company's merit was the quality of the service it provided. Therefore, every policyholder would be treated with the utmost respect, all coverage requests would receive individual attention to detail, and claims would be paid fairly and quickly.

In an early yearly report to policyholders, he wrote, "Everyone from clerks to the president has [done] their utmost to provide prompt and efficient handling of claims, personal service, and careful attention to detail."[6]

Sensing the need for a leader who could bring the prestige of the financial world to the new company, Vigneron recruited Edward P. Metcalf, president of Atlantic National Bank, as the company's first president, while Vigneron himself served as vice president and treasurer, actively directing and managing company operations. Other members of the new company's board included Vigneron's brother, Herbert, and prominent businessmen from the fields of insurance, manufacturing, and utilities.

In the spring of 1907, the Automobile Mutual Insurance Company of America started in modest quarters, with one small room staffed by two clerks at 10 Weybosset Street, a 10-story building then known as "the skyscraper" of Providence.[7] That spring, Vigneron sent out a letter soliciting clients for the new insurance company. He explained that the company had been founded in response to the numerous requests for automobile insurance he had received as assistant secretary at the What Cheer Mutual Fire Insurance Company. He also cautioned prospective policyholders that Amica would not insure automobiles with steam engines (which were far more likely to catch fire). He explained one of the company's founding principles:

We are confining our policyholders to members of the Factory Mutual Insurance Companies, Automobile Clubs in good standing, or persons recommended by responsible parties known to the company. We intend to keep our moral hazard of a high order.

He closed the letter with an invitation to join Amica:

Edward P. Metcalf, first president of Amica, held that office from 1907 to 1910. *(Photo by Fabian Bachrach.)*

Kindly fill out the enclosed blank and return it to us at your earliest convenience, together with the names of such persons in your vicinity whom you would be willing to recommend, and we will see that they are also supplied with blanks.[8]

The automobiles of the day were, by today's standards, extremely expensive. While some could be purchased for around $500, most cost in the range of $2,000 and higher—a considerable amount in 1907. They were also not very powerful, with an average of 20 or 30 horsepower, compared to modern standards of more than 10 times that amount. They were made by a seemingly endless array of car companies, many of which are nearly lost to history: Wintons, Pope–Hartfords, Stevens Duryeas, and Hupmobiles were insured along with Buicks, Fords, and Cadillacs.[9] On March 29, 1907, the Automobile Mutual Insurance Company of

14 AMICA: A CENTURY OF SERVICE 1907–2007

Above: "Mr. A. T." at work in his office, circa 1907.

Left: A letter from Vice President Herbert Vigneron to a potential customer, explaining why Amica couldn't insure automobiles with steam engines.

Opposite: Amica's first application for insurance, covering a 1907 Cadillac originally worth $1,100.

America wrote its first policy, covering a 10-horsepower 1907 Cadillac with an original price of $1,100, owned by Vigneron and his brother, Herbert. The policy was to take effect on April 7.

In the beginning, the company only offered insurance that covered, as Vigneron described it in an early letter, damage to automobiles by "fire, lightning, explosion, theft, and pilferage."[10] Very quickly it became apparent that Vigneron's new concept for an automobile insurance company appealed to a wide audience, and the two clerks at 10 Weybosset Street were kept busy logging handwritten loss reports, staying in touch with claims adjusters, and going through accident reports, some of which came in with the heading "Report of (Horse) Team Accident" with the word "Team" crossed out and "Automobile" written in.

Despite the national financial crisis caused by the Panic of 1907, which precipitated the collapse of many businesses and banks along with plummeting stock prices,[11] by the spring of 1908, Vigneron reported to Amica policyholders:

Our books now show nearly $1 million of insurance, premiums [of] $24,000, and a good surplus; and an amount available for the payment of losses of more than $80,000. Our dividend at present is 25 [percent] of the original premium.

He went on to describe the board of directors and to emphasize to policyholders the concept of preferred risk:

Our board of directors are men of high standing and ability and our members have been selected with care, it being our main object in acquiring business to keep the moral hazard of a high order by requiring references on all applications and, in fact, exercising the same precautions as might be required in any well-regulated society or bonding company.[12]

Finally, as encouraged as he was by Amica's early success, he was even more optimistic about its future:

We are planning to more than double the number of our policyholders this year by requesting our present members to endeavor to procure at least two other applicants, such as they would confidently recommend to insure with us.[13]

The new company was already earning a reputation for excellent service. In June 1908, an executive of the Roxford Knitting Company, manufacturers of men's underwear, wrote to Mr. F. M. Barber, Amica's secretary:

I am pleased to acknowledge receipt of your valued favor of the 19th, with check for $42.09, in payment of claim for loss and damage by fire to my automobile. ... At the sametime [sic], I desire to express to you my appreciation of the prompt manner in which this claim was settled, and shall take great pleasure to recommend your company to any of my friends or acquaintances who may have occasion to place insurance on their automobiles.[14]

For his first year of work, Vigneron took no salary at all. For 1908, his second year, he was paid $300.[15]

The rapid growth of the new insurance company continued. By the end of 1908, Amica had sold nearly $1.3 million in insurance with premiums of close to $34,000. Vigneron reported to his insureds:

We have established during the year ample means for adjusting losses in all territory covered by our policies, and our working force and general system of operation have been brought to the highest point of efficiency. ... All indications point

A postcard illustrating an early Market Square in Providence.

to our ability to increase our dividends in the coming year, which is the best method of advertising that could be suggested.[16]

True to his prediction, the dividend was increased to 30 percent in 1909, and in April 1910, the company sent a postcard to its policyholders announcing, in red ink and capital letters, "ON APRIL 1, 1910, AND UNTIL FURTHER NOTICE, OUR DIVIDEND WILL BE INCREASED TO 35 [percent]."[17]

Vigneron's idea was a great success. He took over as company president in 1910 and in that year's annual report wrote that "well-applied efforts will result in making the year 1911 even more prosperous than the one just closed."[18]

But it is improbable that even he could have foreseen the greater success to come.

The Pace of Change Quickens

For people living in the United States in the first 20 years of the 20th century, the pace at which life was changing due to the rapid development of technology must have been dizzying. The airplane had been invented in 1903; by 1909, a pilot named Louis Blériot had flown 31 miles across the English Channel in only 37 minutes; and in 1910, Glenn Curtiss flew nonstop from Albany to New York City, a distance of 137 miles, in only 152 minutes.[19]

The automobile developed almost as quickly. In 1903, Dr. H. Nelson Jackson and his mechanic, Sewell K. Crocker, made the first-ever cross-country automobile trip in a Winton Motor Carriage, finding along the way that their machine was still very much a curiosity to the people of rural America.[20] In 1908, the great New York to Paris Automobile Race—across the United States to San Francisco, by ship to Japan, across Japan, by ship again to Siberia, and then through Siberia and Russia to Europe—was won by an American and aroused widespread interest in the burgeoning automobile industry. In the words of a magazine editorial of the day: "The automobile has passed entirely out of the plaything stage and is a dependable machine for work as well as pleasure."[21]

In 1911, the first Indianapolis 500 was won at the dazzling average speed of 74.59 miles per hour, and, in that same year, it was estimated that there were 85,000 automobiles on farms alone.[22] The "plaything of the rich," which only a few years before had been limited almost exclusively to urban centers, had now spread across the land.

In 1913, after five years of fine-tuning and testing in search of a more efficient way to make automobiles affordable to the "great multitude," Henry Ford opened the first moving assembly line to produce the Model T automobile. Ford produced automobiles at a record-breaking rate, lowering the price while producing profit by increasing his volume of sales.[23] Ford then took his idea a step further, announcing in the afternoon papers of January 14, 1914, that he was going to pay his employees $5 per eight-hour workday. This more than doubled the national average of $2.50 per nine-hour workday, and soon Ford's workers were buying their own Model Ts. The automobile had been brought within the financial reach of average Americans, and by the summer of 1914, there were 800,000 automobiles rolling along American highways.[24]

Amica, meanwhile, continued its rapid growth. In his president's report for 1913, Vigneron wrote to policyholders that Amica's "ratio, either of Surplus to Premiums or Surplus to Amount at Risk, is larger than that of any other company, either stock or mutual, writing factory fire or automobile insurance."[25] By 1914, the company had written insurance totaling nearly $25 million, with net premiums of well over half a million dollars.[26] Amica had come of age.

Over the years, as the number of automobiles on the road grew and the speed at which they could travel increased, so did the number of accidents involving death, injury, and substantial property damage.[27] Amica received requests for broader insurance coverage from many of its policyholders, and the company directors recognized the need to create an affiliate company responsible for writing various forms of auto liability insurance. A charter incorporating the Factory Mutual Liability Insurance Company of America was issued by the Rhode Island state legislature in January 1914.

The outbreak of World War I, however, caused the substantial disruption of American businesses in 1914, and the Amica board of directors decided that launching a new company in that business climate was too hazardous. As Amica waited for more stable fiscal conditions, efforts to organize the new affiliate continued. In 1916, the foundation for Factory Mutual was firmly set with the election of directors and officers, along with the adoption of company bylaws.[28]

Despite the economic difficulties caused by World War I, America's voracious appetite for automobiles only increased. During the war years, passenger car factory sales nearly doubled, from just under one million in 1915 to nearly two million in 1920. During the same period, privately owned vehicle registrations nearly quadrupled to more than eight million by the end of 1920. Despite the widespread popularity of Fords, there were still some 88 companies manufacturing automobiles at the time. While Ford endured into the next century, competitors such as Halladay, the Briscoe, the Pan-American, and the Apperson eventually fell by the wayside.[29]

Even as Amica increased its volume of business at what must have seemed a staggering rate, it maintained its traditional principles of insuring only carefully selected, "preferred risk" drivers, while concentrating on the delivery of fair settlements and superior customer service. In 1916, Amica

Above: Early automobiles were, by today's standards, slow and expensive.

Left: Before Henry Ford developed the moving assembly line, this car, manufactured in 1894, would have been available only to the rich and powerful.

announced that the dividend to policyholders had been increased to 50 percent—a rate that would continue through 1954—and in his 1917 letter to policyholders, Vigneron wrote: "The President of your Company takes pleasure in announcing that the year 1917 has been the most successful in the history of the Company."[30]

The end of World War I brought significant changes to the social standards, structures, and behavior in America. In 1920, buoyed by their significant contributions to the war effort, women were finally given the right to vote with the passage of the 19th Amendment to the Constitution. Free of wartime anxiety and empowered by shifts in personal wealth caused by higher wages and the end

> ## About the Name Amica
>
> THE MONIKER OF "AMICA" IS SYNONYmous with excellence, integrity, and reliability. For almost a century, it has been used both informally and officially to identify one of the leading insurance companies in the United States.
>
> In 1907, the Automobile Mutual Insurance Company of America was founded. Employees and clients soon began to call this new company by its acronym, "Amica." After the Factory Mutual Liability Insurance Company of America was chartered in 1914 as Automobile Mutual's sister company, the term "Amica companies" became commonly used. In 1973, the two companies merged to form the Amica Mutual Insurance Company, and, after 66 years of casual use, the acronym "Amica" was officially adopted to represent the company.
>
> The name "Amica" has always been liberally employed within the Amica family, and, therefore, this book will concur with this practice by referring to Automobile Mutual and its later affiliation with Factory Mutual as simply "Amica."

of wartime inflation, Americans were not only ready to enjoy themselves, but increasingly had the disposable income to do so.[31] Even the enactment of Prohibition in January 1920 did little to impede the collective respite and celebration known as the Roaring Twenties.

Automated vehicles continued to increase in popularity and in speed, causing an ever-widening demand for automobile insurance across the country. In Providence, Amica readied itself for a decade that would be even more prosperous than the last. The company prepared to launch its long-delayed affiliate, the Factory Mutual Liability Insurance Company of America, and looked to open regional offices beyond the borders of Rhode Island.

In 1920, with Amica firmly established, Vigneron could look back over the 13 years since the founding of the company with good reason to be proud—not only of the company's success, but also of its sterling reputation for fairness and service. He had foreseen that the automobile would become intricately woven into the fabric of American life, and he had proven that the concept of "preferred risk" could be applied to automobile insurance.

Keypunch operators at work at 10 Weybosset Street in the 1930s.

CHAPTER TWO
A Beaten Path to Our Door
1921–1939

Our association is conducted more in the nature of a private club, so selective in character as to make it a privilege to be a member.

—A. T. Vigneron, president of Amica,
in a 1924 letter to policyholders

THE VIGOR OF THE ROARING Twenties emanated from a collective mood of relief and freedom following the grim years of the late teens. Americans shook off the gloomy vestiges remaining from the war years and the influenza pandemic of 1918–1919, which claimed 675,000 lives.[1] Women, having seized the opportunity for increased independence offered to them by wartime work, secured greater political influence when they gained the right to vote. With these advances in structural liberty, women took control of their personal choices as well. Hemlines in the 1920s, for example, would rise to the unprecedented level of just below the knee. Across the country, despite Prohibition, alcohol flowed, and a bold new music, jazz, became popular. People danced, movies entertained, and automobiles streaked in record numbers and at unprecedented speeds across the landscape.

Throughout the 1920s, the pursuit of personal emancipation and postwar vivacity was inexorably linked to the quest of owning an automobile. Not only had cars become, as Vigneron had imagined, part of the fabric of American life, they had also become a potent symbol of freedom and prosperity—of a country on the move. Buyers, then as now, sought in their automobile purchases adventure, social prestige, and pride of ownership. To heighten demand, each year automobile manufacturers created faster, sleeker models; made it easier for people to buy them by creating installment payment plans; and worked around-the-clock to create enough cars to meet demand. In 1924, the 10 millionth Ford produced rolled off the assembly line.

A Partner Company

With the uncertainties of the wartime economy behind them and the favorable business outlook of the early 1920s ahead, the board of directors of Amica elected to activate the Factory Mutual Liability Insurance Company of America, which had been chartered in 1914 but idled during the war years. On January 18, 1921, this second company, managed by directors and officers of Amica who had assumed corresponding positions at the new company, began underwriting automobile liability, property damage, and collision coverage on the same preferred-risk basis as the older company.[2]

The new company was an almost instant success. At the end of its first year, the president's report stated: "Our earnings have been equal to and have even surpassed our expectations," and the new company declared a dividend to its policyholders of 35 percent.[3]

Henry William Anderson, president of Amica from 1933 to 1940.

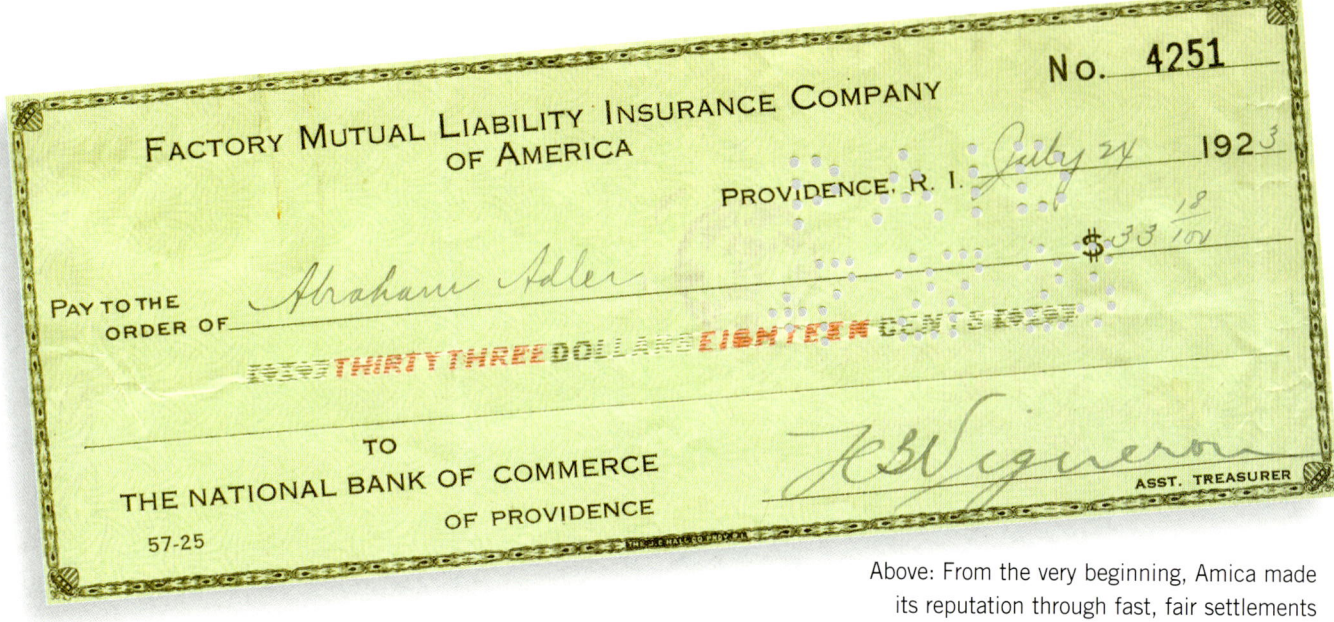

Above: From the very beginning, Amica made its reputation through fast, fair settlements of claims. This check to a policyholder is from 1923.

Left and below: An accident report from 1922.

CHAPTER TWO: A BEATEN PATH TO OUR DOOR

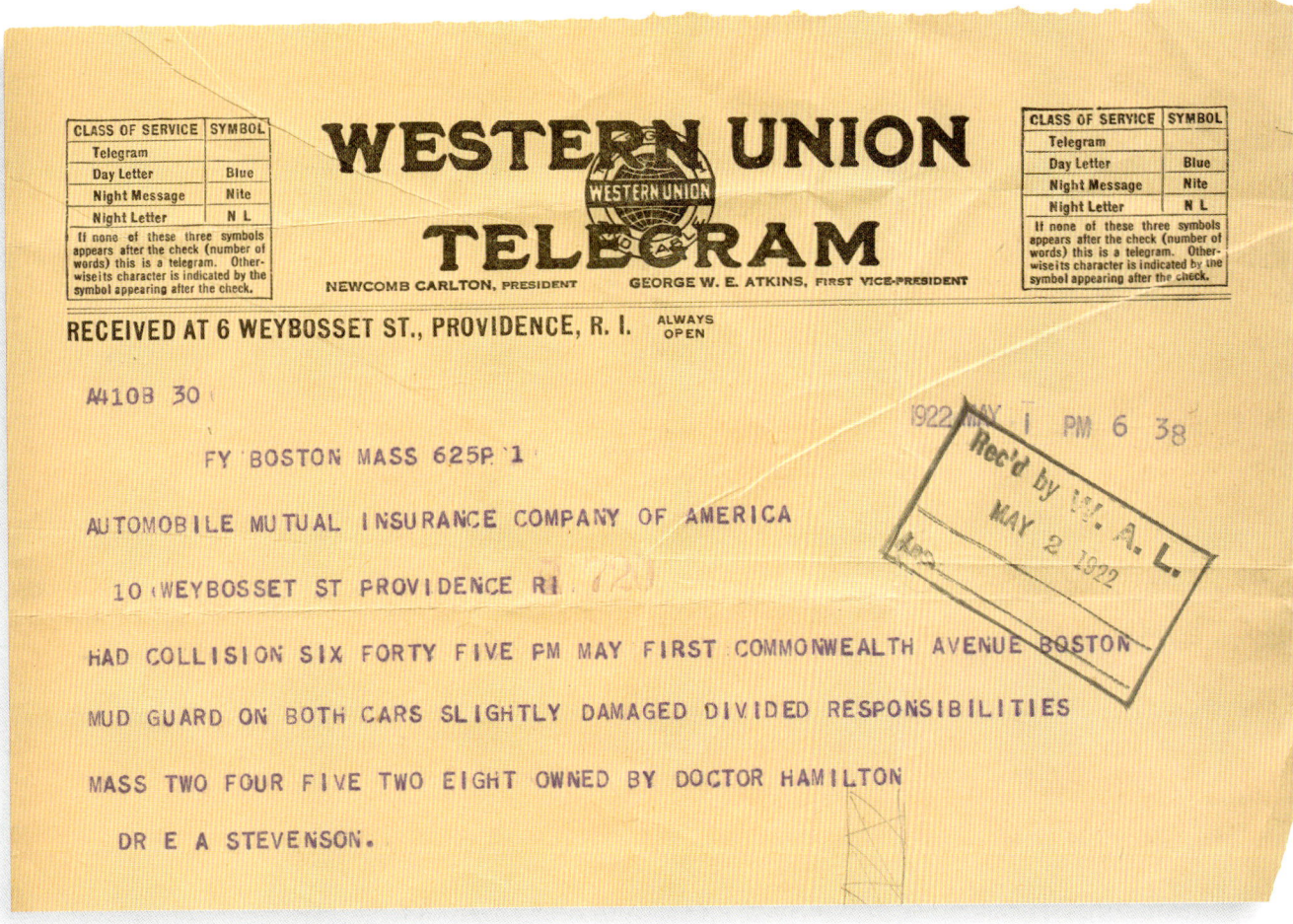

Accident reports often came in by telegram; this one is from May 1922.

In 1922, the Amica companies began to expand across the country, gaining licenses to transact business in Ohio and Massachusetts. That same year, the companies boasted combined assets of more than $1.8 million.

Even amid this incredible growth, under the leadership of Vigneron, the Amica companies remained focused on the ideal of providing the best and most equitable service possible to their customers. Policyholders were the pillars of the company, chosen carefully and entirely looked after once they joined. As Vigneron wrote in a letter to policyholders in 1924: "Please be advised that our association is conducted more in the nature of a private club, so selective in character as to make it a privilege to be a member."[4]

The upstanding nature of the early Amica policyholder is evident in a letter received after an accident in early 1923, in which the policyholder wished to accept the blame for the accident he caused:

January 8th, 1923

From: A. F. Huston, Lukens Steel Company, Coatesville, PA
To: Factory Mutual Liability Insurance Company of America

Sirs:

I wrote to you on the 6th regarding a collision in a fog, stating that the car which collided with my car was on its own side; therefore, I feel that we are responsible for the damages, and the man who owns the other car requires it to get to his work and back again. It has now been fixed up by the Downington Motor Company and a bill rendered

The Amica Christmas parties were among the highlights of the work year, featuring skits, songs, and employee talent shows. This menu is from 1924.

---

for $45.04, which is more than they expected it would be. I have instructed the Downington Motor Company to deliver the car to this man, and I look to you for reimbursement to this amount, the bill for which I herewith enclose. Will you pay the Motor Company direct or through me? Kindly advise.

Yours very truly,
A. F. Huston

Factory Mutual, valuing the integrity of its policyholders, paid the claim promptly.

The annual report for 1924 included a quote from Ralph Waldo Emerson that would remain a kind of motto for Amica for many years to come:

CHAPTER TWO: A BEATEN PATH TO OUR DOOR

If a man can write a better book, preach a better sermon, or make a better mousetrap than his neighbor, though he build his house in the woods, the world will make a beaten path to his door.[5]

This quote not only embodied the company-wide emphasis on service and integrity, but also underscored the idea that Amica did not need soliciting agents to be successful. If the company worked harder than other companies and treated its policyholders better, word of mouth about Amica would spread, and the company would continue to prosper. In a world of increasingly sophisticated selling techniques and advertising, Amica was standing firm on its commitment to provide a quality product above all else.

By the late 1920s, the Amica companies were successful in ways the founders of the companies could not have imagined. By 1927, the combined assets of the Amica companies represented more than $4.5 million. In 1928, both companies changed the way they wrote policies, removing provisions that enabled the companies to assess their policyholders if conditions warranted such assessment.

This signified that Amica had reached a point of financial stability so that policyholders would never be obligated to pay additional money, in excess of premiums, to cover company losses. The previously utilized assessable policies were structured so that policyholders either paid additional money to cover company deficits or received a share of profits, depending on the financial success of the year. However, this custom did not allow the companies to retain adequate reserves to protect against future adversities.

In adopting nonassessable policies, the Amica companies not only implemented a sensible, conservative fiscal philosophy, but also rejuvenated their commitment to putting policyholders first, so that insureds could be secure in the companies' financial soundness. The popularity of these new policies further accelerated the growth of the companies.[6]

Amica was founded on an ironclad commitment to customer service. These Amica employees are hard at work in 1929.

Herbert B. Vigneron, Adolph's brother, was with Amica from the beginning and was president from 1932 to 1933. *(Photo by Fabian Bachrach.)*

Amica Employees Behind the Scenes

As business grew, the number of Amica employees followed suit. From its humble beginnings of two clerks in one small room, Amica had 30 employees occupying half of the ninth floor at 10 Weybosset Street by 1924, and dozens of employees populating several floors of the building by 1929.

Marjorie Sutton, who began her 35-year career with Amica in 1924 at age 19, remembered that the employees worked hard, enjoying both their jobs and camaraderie with fellow employees:

> *When we had Christmas parties—and we always did—we did the entertaining. We had plays, skits, musicals, and lots of fun. Some of us wrote the scripts, usually Miss Faust, Mr. See, or myself! The desks were cleared away from the back of the room on the sixth floor, and we danced, too. We were a family—a loyal, happy family.*[7]

Sutton's first interview was with Henry Anderson, then-secretary of the company, who would become president a few years later. She then passed dictation and typewriting tests before being introduced to Herbert B. Vigneron and, a few minutes later, A. T. Vigneron himself. The young woman impressed the three company officers enough that they offered her a job, earning $80 a month.[8]

Amica employees received bonuses at the end of the year, usually 15 percent of their annual salary paid in a lump sum, and yearly raises of usually $5 or $10 a month. One year, a $15 a month raise put Sutton in "seventh heaven!"[9]

As the Amica companies experienced even greater success in the years to come, they maintained an ironclad commitment to customer service. Sutton, who eventually married and took the name Chace, wrote of Amica's early days:

> *We maintained our reputation of being one of the most dependable, most selective, most considerate insurance companies in the country. Oh heck, we thought we were the best.*[10]

From the beginning, the relationship between policyholders and staff was highly valued, and Amica went to great lengths so that policyholders were familiarized with the growing staff of the companies. To this end, Amica included in its 1929 annual report photographs of the Amica offices. As Adolph Vigneron wrote in his letter to policyholders that year:

> *To acquaint policyholders and prospects with the personnel of our home office, we have incorporated in this booklet photographs illustrating the various departments that take part in the underwriting of the policies which we issue.*[11]

The photographs depicted employees in various departments sitting in rows of extremely tidy desks and hard at work. Well-dressed and professional, these men and women appeared to be fully concentrated on the tasks at hand. The pictures not only offered policyholders a chance to survey Amica's office environment, but provided a sense of Amica's reliability and efficiency.

The Crash of 1929 and Leadership Changes

The burst of exuberance that permeated American society in the 1920s took the stock market by storm. A decade-long boom raised stock prices to record levels; between 1920 and 1929 stocks more than quadrupled in value, and many investors, convinced that stocks were a sure thing, borrowed heavily to invest more money in the market.[12] The stock bubble swelled even more dangerously in the final years of the decade, with the Dow Jones Industrial Average going from 191 in early 1928, to 300 by December of that year, and an astounding 381 by September 1929.[13] In October, however, the Dow began to slide, and between October 29, known as Black Tuesday, and November 13, when stock prices reached the lowest point of the crisis, more than $30 billion disappeared from the American economy.[14] By early 1933, stocks were down about 80 percent from their height in the late 1920s.[15]

The crash of 1929 helped trigger the Great Depression of the 1930s, and the U.S. economy would take years to recover. During this era, automobile production declined greatly. The Amica companies, however, continued to grow, increasing their number of policyholders each year even in the midst of the Great Depression.[16] While the Depression would leave very few business organizations unscathed, Amica's focus on sound, conservative investment policies successfully brought the companies through the difficult period.[17]

Sutton remembered:

During the stock market crash of 1929 and the Depression, we found that our investments had been carefully and conservatively made and that we were still on a solid foundation. I remember that when many companies were reducing their working staffs, we were still receiving our modest yearly raises.

In the midst of the Depression, the Amica companies were hit with another difficult challenge with the death of the companies' founder, Adolph T. Vigneron. According to the historical book *Pathway of Progress*, published by Amica in celebration of the company's 50th anniversary in 1957, Vigneron was a "leader of great vision, a business associate of kindly personality, [and] a friend of sincere understanding."[18] He had led the companies for more than 20 years before succumbing to a heart ailment in October 1931 at the age of 64.

In a poignant reminder of his goodwill and the determination with which he had always treated his own lifelong handicap of limited mobility, Vigneron left more than $250,000 for the establishment of a trust

---

Below left: The ratings and valuations department, circa 1929. *(Photo by Paine Studios.)*

Below right: The calm, professional atmosphere of the claims department was depicted for policyholders in the 1929 annual report.

in memory of his mother "for the purpose of supplying appropriate treatment and appliances for [handicapped] children and adults, who are residents of the State of Rhode Island, children to have preference."[19]

In February 1932, Vigneron's brother, Herbert, succeeded him as president of the companies. "Mr. H. B." had been co-owner with his brother of the very first automobile insured and had served the company as vice president and treasurer for many years, often helping his brother with many of the tasks that Adolph's physical disability prevented him from doing himself. Yet Herbert Vigneron's tenure as president lasted slightly less than a year. In January 1933 he, too, died of a heart condition.[20]

The following month, Henry William Anderson, a self-made, self-educated executive who had earned a reputation for outstanding character and hard work while ascending the business ladder, was elected president of the companies. Anderson had played a prominent role in the development of the second Amica company, the Factory Mutual Liability Insurance Company of America, and in helping Amica endure during the years of the Depression.[21] His shrewd business sense and practical abilities would prove an excellent match for Amica, as the companies continued to grow.

In his first letter to policyholders, who might have been concerned by the deaths of the Vigneron brothers and the weakened American economy, Anderson reported large gains in assets and a surplus for the year just completed. He dispatched a reassuring note:

During the year, every effort was made to conduct the business of the Companies in a most conservative manner; efficiency, however, being stressed always. The success of the Companies depends wholly upon the merits of the service which we render to policyholders. Having no personal representatives to contact the prospects, much consideration is given to the effort of satisfying the insured and thereby encouraging them to recommend our proposition to their friends. The consistent growth of the Companies, even during the recent years of depression, shows the results of this consideration.[22]

CHAPTER TWO: A BEATEN PATH TO OUR DOOR

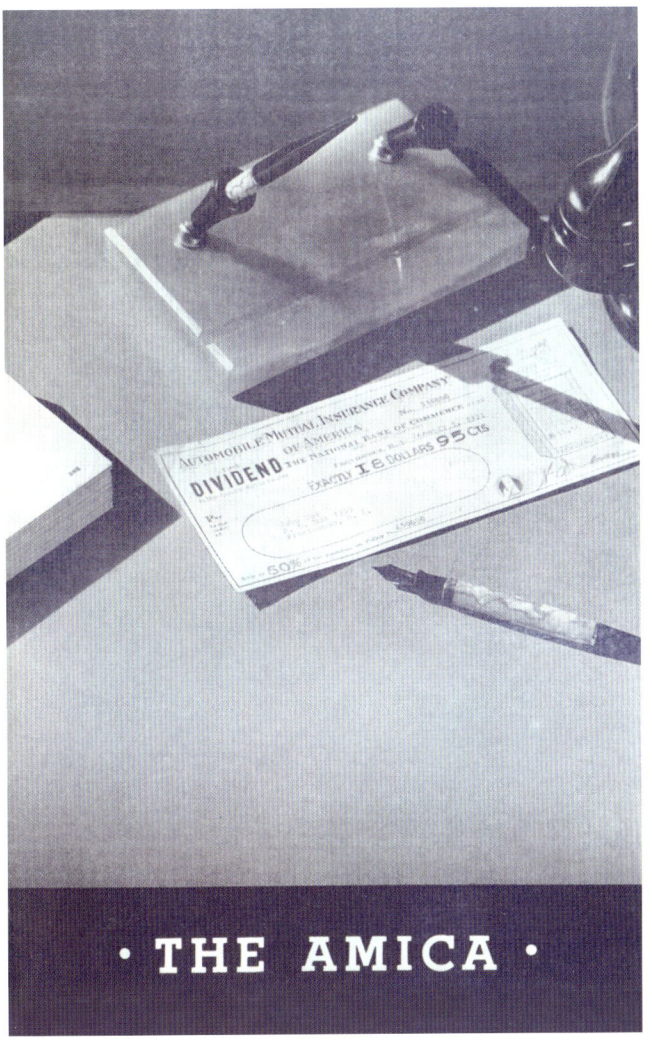

This page and opposite: Amica annual reports from 1932 to 1935.

In 1934, Anderson wrote a letter to policyholders, titled "Those Four Long Years," in which he addressed the difficulties of the Great Depression:

Sooner or later in the life of every business organization must come a test of sound management and basic stability. There is no doubt that American business enterprises of all kinds have been severely tried during the past four years—a period of general deflation and sub-normal conditions which has no parallel within the lifetime of most of us. We, who have had great faith in the principles upon which our associations are built and operated, have watched with anxious eyes the tide of business affairs. And the outcome of these years of hardship has been one in which we take a keen and pardonable pride.

Anderson took extra care to reassure policyholders that, although Amica had lost its founder and the economy was still in crisis, the company would be run by the same principles that had created great success. His strong leadership and keen understanding of what made Amica special—why so many policyholders, in the words of Emerson, "make a beaten path" to Amica's door—helped to usher the companies on to new successes.

1930s—Beginning of a New Era

Throughout the 1920s, as the American economy prospered, the practice of installment buying, or "buying on time," brought automobiles within

The cast of the Amica Christmas party play in 1936. *(Photo by Amil Studios.)*

the financial reach of millions of Americans. Thirteen million cars were bought on installment plans during the decade, and, in the early 1930s, Amica decided to offer low-cost automobile financing to policyholders. The new company, Amica Credit Corporation, was founded in 1936 and was an immediate success, quickly expanding its operations to provide financing in all the New England states, New York, and New Jersey. The smoothness with which the Amica Credit Corporation was launched and expanded further demonstrated the managerial skill of Amica.[23]

In 1933, the 21st Amendment to the Constitution was passed, repealing the national prohibition of alcohol that had been in effect since the ratification of the 18th Amendment in 1920. Whether Prohibition had ever done much to stop people from drinking is debatable. As historian Peter McWilliams noted, Prohibition actually allowed organized crime to grow into an empire and tempted police, judges, and politicians to become increasingly corrupt. At the same time, disrespect for the law grew, and the per capita consumption of alcohol actually increased dramatically year by year.

One of the most telling examples of Prohibition's failure came in 1926 when Russell Post, a student at Yale University, testified before a Senate committee about the effects of Prohibition on the Yale community. The proceedings turned to the issue of whether students were able to obtain liquor:

> *Mr. Post: Why, it is obtainable, sir; the greater the attempts at enforcement the stronger the sentiment against it.*
>
> *Senator Reed of Missouri: Do bootleggers ply their trade among the students?*
>
> *Mr. Post: Well, it is the reverse; the students go to the bootleggers.*

By 1931, a presidential committee appointed to investigate the effectiveness of Prohibition agreed it was a failure. In 1932, both candidates for president, Franklin D. Roosevelt and Herbert Hoover, favored the repeal of Prohibition, and on December 5, 1933, the 18th Amendment was repealed.

Whether or not the legalization of alcohol was felt directly on the nation's highways and roads is unclear, but the increased number of cars on the roads and the increased speeds at which those cars traveled meant a rise in the number of car accidents. In the 1933 annual report, Amica President Anderson wrote of the automobile: "It is sad to reflect that one of the greatest conveniences of the century is rapidly becoming one of the greatest menaces to human life."[24]

Anderson was well aware of the changing landscape of American transportation. In 1934, he reflected on the transformation of the automobile industry and its impact on Amica in a letter to policyholders titled, "1907 Up to Today":

Twenty-seven years has witnessed a great change in motoring. It's a far cry from tonneaux that buttoned up the back and engine hoods that opened down the front to streamlines and knee action and no-draft ventilation. It's considerably more than that from the era of dusters and veils and goggles to motor radios, electric clocks, and tricky cigar lighters. And the difference between a terrifying 15 miles an hour then and a somewhat conservative 40 today is a bit bewildering to think about. One thing that hasn't changed during this period is the need for insurance protection, except to increase with the growing hazards of the road.[25]

Anderson also praised Vigneron and the other founders of the company for having had the foresight to recognize the future need for an insurance company such as Amica:

Back in 1907, a group of men laid the foundation for these associations. They probably had no idea that its growth would be so great or its success so notable, but they laid a good foundation.[26]

In the annual report for 1934, Anderson set his agenda for the coming years by reiterating the importance of service, a cornerstone of Amica:

We regard service to our policyholders as just about the most important factor in our business. ... The very fact that we have no salesmen or solicitors or branch offices imposes upon us an obligation to develop a service organization that is able to render swift and satisfactory service to every policyholder.

Lacking an elaborate and costly chain of branch offices, we have developed a service system that has enabled us to render not just ordinary service to our members, but service of a sort that fills our files with letters from satisfied people who write us voluntarily to tell us of their pleasure and who invariably choose such a time to recommend new members.[27]

In 1934, Anderson would report that the Amica companies' cash assets had increased to $3.7 million. While the Great Depression was not yet over, Amica had weathered its first true tests.

In 1937, Amica celebrated the 30th anniversary of its founding. Anderson contemplated how far the company and the automobile industry had come:

Thirty years ago, when Amica service began, there were many people, and by no means ignorant folks at that, who regarded the automobile as a devil-inspired invention [that] would do more harm

The popularity of cars often outstripped the availability of roads. Here a motorist grapples with the results.

CONDENSED ANNUAL STATEMENTS, DECEMBER 31, 1939
AS FILED WITH THE INSURANCE DEPARTMENTS OF THE STATE OF RHODE ISLAND AND WASHINGTON, D. C.

Automobile Mutual Insurance Company of America
Providence, R. I.

ASSETS

U. S. Government Bonds and Notes	$2,269,855.80
State, Municipal, and Dominion of Canada Bonds	375,156.83
Public Utilities and other Bonds and Stocks	1,616,285.32
Cash on hand and in Banks	284,948.58
Other admitted assets	39,692.05
TOTAL ASSETS	**$4,585,938.58**

LIABILITIES

Losses in process of adjustment	$ 6,419.00
Reserve for unearned premiums	337,842.11
All other liabilities	47,681.32
Voluntary reserve	350,000.00
TOTAL LIABILITIES	**$741,942.43**
SURPLUS TO POLICYHOLDERS	$3,843,996.15
(Including Guarantee Fund $250,000.00)	

"Securities carried at $247,200.00 in the above statement are deposited as required by law"

Factory Mutual Liability Insurance Company of America
Providence, R. I.

ASSETS

U. S. Government Bonds and Notes	$9,115,503.46
State, Municipal, and Dominion of Canada Bonds	539,883.48
Public Utilities and other Bonds and Stocks	1,684,306.62
Cash on hand and in Banks	1,537,216.33
Other admitted assets	86,179.21
TOTAL ASSETS	**$12,963,089.10**

LIABILITIES

Reserves for unpaid losses	$2,950,904.06
Reserve for unearned premiums	1,037,215.25
All other liabilities	421,507.83
State of New York special reserve	100,000.00
Voluntary reserve	1,000,000.00
TOTAL LIABILITIES	**$5,509,627.14**
SURPLUS TO POLICYHOLDERS	$7,453,461.96
(Including Guarantee Fund $250,000.00)	

"Securities carried at $252,600.00 in the above statement are deposited as required by law"

All the securities owned by these Companies were valued on the basis approved by the National Association of Insurance Commissioners

---

than good in the world. It was not by any means unusual in those days to find men and women who would not ride in any such contraption and who could prove to you with deep feeling and earnest conviction that the horse could never be replaced by any form of mechanical transportation.

Theodore Roosevelt was in the White House. United States Army engineers were blasting their way through the Isthmus of Panama. Tops, windshields, and luggage carriers were extra luxuries. And here and there along the narrow, rough country roads, boys would yell, "Git a horse," to the begoggled and dustered driver who sat grimly behind the wheel.

Thirty years later, this is an era of streamlined, super-powered motorcars, four- and six-lane highways [and] speed, comfort, luxury, and economy, which would have seemed fantastic in 1907. Amica protection and service are being rendered to thousands and thousands of motorcar owners in nearly every state in the Union. But they are still selected and are still preferred risks who have been invited to become members of these associations.[28]

That same year, 1937, Larry Tingley, a young man fresh from college, began what would eventually be a 43-year career with Amica by taking a job in what was then known as the rating department. The department was located on the fifth floor of the skyscraper at 10 Weybosset Street and was responsible for rating renewals and new business orders.

Every year, Amica sent a condensed annual statement to its policyholders—the people who own the company. This one from 1939 shows Amica's early success.

Tingley immediately felt at home within Amica, as the values upheld in the office reflected his own morals, learned while growing up in Rhode Island.

"I thought the culture of Amica was good because it was the way I was brought up," he said. "I took pride in being part of a company that had a regard for its policyholders and treated them the way they would expect to be treated, ... with patience and skill."[29]

Tingley enjoyed his job and his coworkers, who were a close-knit group. He looked forward to the yearly Christmas parties and felt good dressing in a dignified way for work each day. He recalled that "Amica employees were not only pretty nice, but they were all substantial and respectful people."

The patience and skill Tingley referred to were evident in a passage from the 1937 annual report titled, "Speaking of Claims: Amica's Superintendent of Claims Has a Word to Say." Describing a typical working day in the claims department at Amica, the report illustrated employees' commitment to policyholders:

The telephone rings. One of our members en route to Florida has had an accident somewhere in Tennessee. ... A telegram from somewhere in Pennsylvania. Our member has run off the road, struck a tree and is in a hospital; likewise, his two passengers. Our representative is in touch with him immediately, and the investigation is under way within an hour.

Here in the Home Office, our work constantly demands quick action. We have our fingers on the pulse of the world, in a sense, and it keeps us on our mettle to be ready to cope with any situation. There is a lot of romance in our work ... romance and stiff, stark tragedy, too. We meet both humor and pathos, and we have become specialists in the understanding of human nature through having to meet and deal with claimants with all sorts of traits, both good and bad.

Ours is the responsibility not only of seeing that investigations are inaugurated promptly and carried out fully, but of keeping constantly in mind the welfare of our members. We try in every possible way to minimize the trouble and inconvenience that are usually associated with accidents.

In 1938, Amica continued to grow, adding residential, general liability, and burglary coverage to its insurance offerings.

On September 21 of that year, the Amica companies faced the biggest test yet of their ability to provide swift and fair service when a catastrophic hurricane hit Rhode Island. Winds reached more than 100 miles per hour and drove a tidal wave into downtown Providence, flooding the business district, including the Amica Home Office, to a depth of 13 feet.[30]

Tingley, who was at work at 10 Weybosset Street that day, recalled the scene:

The water came over the top and flooded downtown Providence, but I got out before that on one of the last buses to leave Providence before South Main Street was flooded. I got as far home as the six corners in East Providence, and then the buses stopped running. Out of curiosity, I walked back to downtown Providence to see what it was like, since I thought the water had probably gone down. The water had receded, and I could see all right. People were looting down there.[31]

By the time the hurricane blew through, 262 people were killed and property damage was estimated at more than $100 million. Hundreds of homes were damaged or destroyed, and flood damage to automobiles was "enormous." The Amica companies received more than 1,000 claims, which were handled in the company's usual prompt and fair way.[32]

At the next annual meeting, President Anderson reported that:

The treatment of the insured was apparently well received, as we have heard many favorable comments both directly and indirectly concerning the matter, and if considered from a profit and loss viewpoint, we are of the opinion that the Company will be well repaid because of the goodwill thus created.[33]

Larry Tingley took pride in how his company had handled the awful hurricane. "The way they recovered from the 1938 hurricane was certainly something [that] created a lot of goodwill and made the public respect Amica," he said.[34]

In 1939, as the Amica companies continued to grow, Anderson oversaw the adoption of a liberal pension plan for all Amica employees, the costs of which were borne entirely by the companies.[35]

As the decade of the 1930s drew to a close, Amica had survived its first severe tests. Its experience with adversity would provide a solid grounding for the company in the next decade—a decade that would bring continued growth to Amica and great change in the world.

During World War II, Amica contributed to the war effort in every possible way. This company-sponsored billboard in Providence, Rhode Island, urged people to buy war bonds. The 10 Weybosset Street building, where Amica began, is the one pictured middle left. *(Photo by David Davidson.)*

CHAPTER THREE

FROM COAST TO COAST
1940–1950

The events attendant upon World War II made the handling of our business increasingly difficult. ... The manufacture of automobiles was greatly curtailed, ... many of our trained men and women entered the armed services and defense industries, ... and then, when the war was over, there were the many post-war problems to be dealt with. Notwithstanding all these trying conditions, the progress of the Companies has been ever forward!

—DeForest W. Abel, 1950 annual report

AS THE 1940s DAWNED, THE world was transitioning from a decade of severe economic depression into what appeared to be even more uncertain times. The German invasion of Poland on September 1, 1939, had pushed an already tense Europe to the brink of world war. While England and France prepared to fight, Germany marched on, conquering Norway, Denmark, Luxembourg, Holland, and Belgium. When Germany invaded France in May 1940, Europe became fully engulfed in World War II.

With the memory of the First World War all too fresh in their minds, many Americans wanted the United States to stay out of what they viewed as a European conflict. Yet, even as Americans debated whether or not to become actively engaged in the fight, there was a strong sentiment in support of helping their British allies with arms and equipment. The war clouds gradually spread toward the United States.

During the first months of 1940, employees at Amica also experienced another kind of uncertainty. In January 1940, Henry Anderson, the president of the company, died at age 54 after a yearlong illness. While Anderson had served as president for fewer than eight years, he had been with the company for many years as secretary.

His knowledge of the casualty insurance business, as well as his outstanding ability as an administrator, greatly influenced the sound and steady development of Amica. Under his leadership, during the difficult economic conditions of the 1930s, the assets of the two companies increased from $10.8 million to $17.5 million—an outstanding record.[1] On the day of his funeral, the Amica offices were closed, and all employees attended the ceremony.[2]

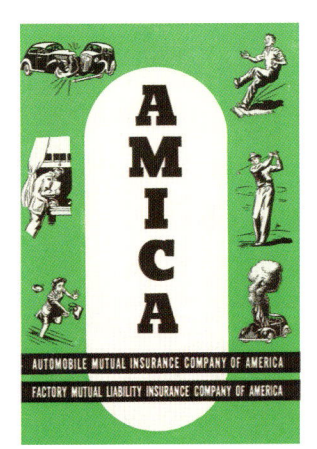

Anderson was replaced as president by DeForest W. Abel, a 14-year veteran of the company whose status among other employees as a relative "newcomer" reflected the stability and respect for tradition within Amica's culture. Abel's formidable talents had distinguished him from his first day at the company.

Abel was born in Franklin, Tennessee, in 1890 and grew up in Ithaca, New York. He attended Cornell University, where he earned a law degree, and, in 1916, began his insurance career with the General Accident Fire and Life Insurance Corporation in Philadelphia. He served in the military during World War I and after the war joined a Boston insurance company as a solicitor and branch man-

---

The 1945 annual report contained stories from Amica employees serving in the armed forces in Italy, the Philippines, France, and on the home front.

While the front page of the October 20, 1942, edition of *The Boston Post* reports the news from the Pacific front of World War II, an advertisement bought by a group of automobile insurance companies appearing on page 2 announces the refund of more than $3 million in insurance premiums. Gasoline rationing and other wartime restrictions curtailed driving, lessening the risks associated with operating a vehicle.

---

ager. In 1926, Abel accepted a position as an adjuster with Amica and in 1928 was appointed assistant secretary. By 1933, he was secretary of the company, and by 1939, vice president. In 1940, Abel capped his meteoric rise through the organization when he was named president.[3]

One Amica employee, Gardiner Northup, remembered Abel's first day as president. On February 13, 1940, Northup, a recent high school graduate, came in for a job interview. He was sitting in the vice president's office, not sure if he had been hired yet, waiting for the new company president to come out of his own office. When Abel came out, he extended a hand to Northup. "I'm glad to meet you," Abel said. "Now we're both starting on a new job today."

Northup then knew that he was hired. He stayed at Amica until 1980 and remembered his early days at the company with great fondness:

> *When I first came to Amica, we had one-and-a-half floors of the Amica Building in Providence, which was called the Grosvenor Building. There were maybe 30 or 40 employees working at the company at that time. So we were like a big family. After work, we would have our roller skating parties, or we would get together, bowling, things of that sort. We were like a big family, and everybody knew one another.*[4]

Among Abel's first projects as president was the development of the Amica acronym and its establishment as a registered trademark—an innovation that would not become popular throughout the insurance industry until the 1970s.[5] Abel also strove to carry on "without change [to] the policies of management, which had proved so successful" over the years.[6]

In November 1941, the new president embarked on an era of countrywide expansion, showcasing a "new corporate strategy for growth with the added advantage of affording better local policyholder service" by opening Amica's first branch office in Boston.[7]

Another Level of Service

As Amica continued to grow throughout 1940 and 1941, so did the number of fatalities on America's highways. With thoughts of the war raging in Europe and Asia never far from anyone's mind, Abel drew parallels in his "Message to Our Members," for the 1941 annual report, between the horrific atrocities of war and the needless tragedies on American roadways. He urged readers to consider deaths from car accidents in the same light in which they considered the grim news from Europe and to, therefore, drive more carefully:

> *We are all moved when we pick up our daily newspaper or turn on our radio and learn of the needless death and destruction caused by the bombing of innocent non-combatants. In London, during the first two months of this year, 2,291 people were killed by bombs. During this same period, over 5,000 were killed in this country as a result of automobile accidents.*[8]

The war clouds of 1940 and 1941 finally burst over the United States on December 7, 1941, when

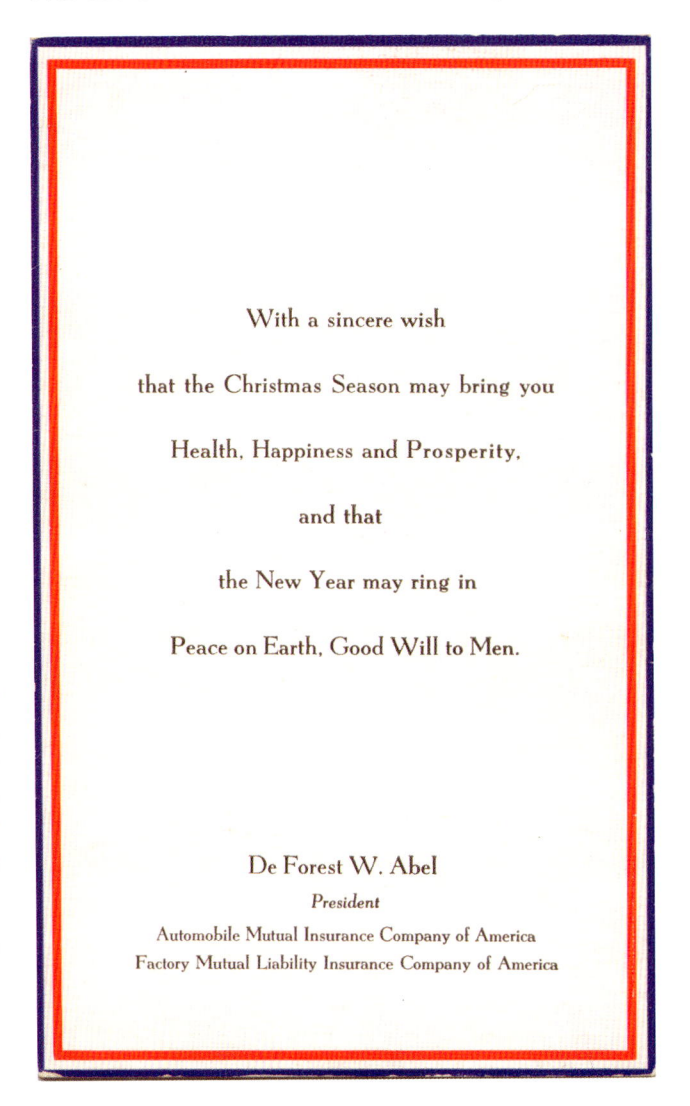

At the end of the United States' first year of fighting in World War II, Amica's Christmas card from 1942 expresses hope for peace in the coming year.

With a sincere wish

that the Christmas Season may bring you

Health, Happiness and Prosperity,

and that

the New Year may ring in

Peace on Earth, Good Will to Men.

De Forest W. Abel

President

Automobile Mutual Insurance Company of America

Factory Mutual Liability Insurance Company of America

Crippled Liberator with Local Pilot Returns from Solo Raid on Berlin

LT. A. V. PEARSON DEFEATS CONKED ENGINE

Bomber Pushes Through Alone to Complete Its Mission; Flak Heavy

"Well, I'm certainly glad to see Albert in the news for a change, instead of my other son, John," said Mrs. George M. Pearson of 66 Dorman avenue, North Providence, when informed last night that her son had piloted a Liberator, with one engine out, on to Berlin Monday and safely back to England despite heavy flak and a 30-minute attack by German fighters.

John—Staff Sergeant John T. Pearson—flight engineer of an Army B-24, made the headlines for his daring in the South Pacific from January to November of last year, in the course of which he won the Silver Star, the Distinguished Flying Cross, Air Medal and Purple Heart awards. He was wounded seven times in a one-plane attack on Wewak, and is now in a base hospital in Atlantic City.

Albert—Lt. Albert V. Pearson, 26—also made a one-plane attack on Berlin Monday. A troublesome engine on "Lil Max," the Liberator he piloted, conked out while still 40 miles from the target in the first United States raid on the Reich capital.

Pearson couldn't keep up with his formation, and other crewmen in the group gave "Lil Max" up for lost, figuring that alone it could never weather the tough Nazi opposition.

One man in what had been Pearson's group, described visibility as "two-tenths cloud and eight-tenths flak." But the North Providence man took "Lil Max" on into Berlin, and her bomb load was dropped on the target, as an unexpected anti-climax to the concerted raids.

"Lil Max" turned for home, fought through the flak, beat off fighter planes and made it to England, even though she had no escort until she was back over Holland, the Associated Press reported.

Mrs. Pearson at first clasped her hands nervously last night when informed there was news of her son in a cable from England. When she learned a moment later he was safe and that his exploit had put him in the headliner class with John, she then expressed her satisfaction, figuring it was time for the older son to "win some notice." Albert's father also was pleased at the news of the safe return of "Lil Max."

The mother said Lt. Pearson enlisted Aug. 10, 1942. He won his wings at Blackland Field, Waco, Tex., May 5, 1943, and went overseas last October. His mother last saw him in September of last year, just before he sailed.

"Why I just got a letter Monday, and was reading it while he was doing all this crippled flying," the mother said.

"He writes almost every day, but he never gives me any news of what he's doing—just sends copies of The Stars and Stripes to take care of that. He's a first lieutenant, you know. Promoted five weeks ago. I guess they knew what they were doing, promoting him."

Lieut. Pearson attended North Providence elementary schools and was graduated from Hope high school. Before enlisting he was employed as a bookkeeper by an auto insurance company in Providence.

He has written that bookkeeping is a little tame compared with missions over Germany.

Lt. Albert V. Pearson

This article from the *Providence Evening Bulletin* in 1944 tells the remarkable survival story of Lt. Albert V. Pearson, an Amica employee who conducted a solo air raid on Berlin during World War II. Pearson would work for Amica for almost 50 years and serve on Amica's board of directors. *(Photo courtesy of The Providence Journal.)*

---

the Japanese attacked Pearl Harbor. The attack solidified American resolve and called the young men and women of what would become the "Greatest Generation" to the fight against tyranny. In the 1942 annual report, Abel wrote:

> *We are now in the midst of a gigantic war, the like of which the world has never seen. It profoundly affects every one of us and our very way of life. ... Our first consideration is to win the war. To attain victory we will have to change many of our everyday habits. Sacrifices will be required from everybody, including the motorist. ...*
>
> *Modern warfare cannot function without rubber, and our supply of rubber is limited. It therefore behooves each and every motorist to conserve in every way possible our greatest stockpile of rubber, which is represented by the tires on the country's 30,000,000 automobiles. Unnecessary driving must be eliminated and speeds reduced, in order to prolong the life of our present tires and maintain intact our transportation system. ... Speed our war effort by driving slowly and carefully.*[9]

Amica did not just urge sacrifices from its policyholders; the company contributed to the war effort in every way possible, and, over the course of the war, Amica employees served their country well. In 1944, Abel wrote to policyholders:

> *Since our Country has been at war, we, like all other business concerns, have been confronted with a multitude of problems, our chief one being loss of personnel. We have a record of not asking for a single deferment from military service for anyone in our employ since the war started. Fifty percent of our male employees are now in some branch of the Armed Services of our Country, being stationed all over the globe. In addition, a number of our women employees have voluntarily joined the WAVES, the WAC, the SPARs, and the Marines.*[10]

Amica employees indeed served all over the world. One of Amica's employees made headlines for his participation in the first American daylight bombing raid over Berlin. While still 40 miles from the target, Albert Pearson's B-24 Liberator experienced mechanical problems, forcing him to fall behind his formation. Even with one engine out, Pearson completed the mission, essentially carrying out an unexpected solo raid on Berlin. According to the *Providence Evening Bulletin*, Pearson provided "an unexpected anti-climax to the concerted raids ... despite heavy flak and a 30-minute attack by German fighters."

Many employees served with distinction. Gardiner Northup would become one of the original crew members on the battleship USS *Missouri*, serving at Iwo Jima, Okinawa, and the Philippines. He was aboard the *Missouri* when the Japanese surrender was signed on September 2, 1945.[11] Another young man took part in the invasion of the Marshall Islands on January 31, 1944. Several female employees served in the U.S. Coast Guard Women's Reserve, also know as the SPARs. Amica sadly lost one employee, Alexander M. MacLachlan, when he was killed in combat on December 6, 1944.[12]

Stories from servicemen and women stationed in Italy, France, the Philippines, and other countries were reprinted in Amica's communications with policyholders. Their letters home painted compelling pictures of hardships, suffering, and a renewed appreciation for life. The overriding message in these reports was clear: Amica unequivocally supported employees' sacrifices for the country and their contributions to the war effort. The 1944 annual report stated:

[On the home front], there is hardly a phase of the ... war effort that is not being aided by the generous, unstinting offers of help by Amica workers. Many have joined in direct war production work—performing the special tasks for the war for which they are best suited. Our personnel serve in a hundred and one volunteer capacities; in Civilian Defense; in the Red Cross; as blood donors; as canteen hostesses; as war bond campaign workers.

While this is the sort of response that SHOULD be found in every American company in wartime, we are proud of the job our boys and girls are doing—proud that they are the sort who will not shirk their responsibilities.[13]

Business During the War

Running the companies during World War II presented many unique challenges. To begin with, Amica became a fiduciary agent of the War Damage Corporation (WDC), insuring homes of policyholders against damage through enemy action. Furthermore, the large number of Amica employees serving in the armed forces put a strain on the company's ability to provide the customer service for which it was so well known. In 1944, Abel explained:

The loss of such a large percentage of employees [to military service], many of whom were in key positions, has made it difficult for us to render at all times as fast service as would be the case under normal conditions. Notwithstanding the handicap under which we are operating today, we are endeavoring to render fast, efficient, friendly service. The cooperation and understanding of our policyholders during this trying period is very much appreciated.[14]

Abel's focus on maintaining high standards of customer service did not waver. Northup, who worked in the mailroom in the early 1940s, noted:

Our rule was, every letter we received from an insured, we had to answer. This was Mr. Abel's rule. That letter had to be answered within 24 hours. No delays. No excuses. If you needed to stay all night doing the mail, you did it. Twenty-four hours later, that letter had to be answered, and we did it.[15]

The scarcity of many materials presented particular difficulties to the automotive industry. Rubber was scarce; tires and gasoline were rationed; and, in order to devote all available resources to the war effort, car companies were not able to produce new models during the war years. In 1943, roughly 98 percent of Amica's dealings involved automobile insurance. Abel reassured policyholders that despite the reduction in driving, loss ratios were "satisfactory," while business was proceeding on a "very sound basis."[16]

Of course, natural disasters did not stop occurring because the country was at war. In September 1944, a hurricane lashed New England with "mountainous seas and furious winds," causing millions of dollars in property damage. Short-handed or not, the companies settled all claims promptly and fairly, as they always had.[17]

Back to Business

Even beset by the difficulties of operating in a wartime economy, Amica continued to grow. After the war ended, the servicemen and women returned to their jobs, new cars poured off assembly lines, and Amica began another period of sustained, intensive expansion. The extensive development of the nation's transportation infrastructure included plans to build highways bridging every region and state in the country, as well as connecting to major roadways in Canada and Mexico. In 1946, Congress proposed joint federal–state expenditures of $1.5 billion over the first three postwar years.[18]

After the war, Amica experienced significant organizational growth and maturity. On January 1, 1946, the first group of employees retired under the pension plan that had been started in 1939. Also in 1946, Amica acquired control of the entire office building at 10 Weybosset Street, where the company began. It opened its second branch office in Springfield, Massachusetts, and was licensed to do business in every state in the continental United States and the District of Columbia.[19]

By 1947, Amica's 40th anniversary, the companies boasted assets in excess of $24 million.[20] A "Victory Dinner" was held in October of that year to honor employees who had served during the war and to celebrate the companies' 40th year. Amica presented gold discharge buttons to veterans and awarded employees who had been with the company for a quarter-century or more with 25-year service pins. A bronze service plaque bearing the names of Amica veterans was unveiled in the lobby of the sixth floor of the Home Office building at 10 Weybosset Street in downtown Providence. Subsequent to a speech by Abel, a social hour was held, followed by more speeches, music, and a dinner featuring roast sirloin of beef.

Amica had grown to become one of the leading insurance companies in the country. With nearly 350 employees, occupying 30,000 square feet of office floor space, Amica issued approximately 150,000 policies in 1947 and was close to reaching an annual income of $5 million.[21] This growth was especially impressive considering that most new policyholders came to join the company on the recommendation of current and former members.

Life at the Home Office

Even as the ranks of Amica employees swelled in the late 1940s, the company held fast to its commitment to provide superior customer service and maintain a traditional office environment, which were so integral to its success. At a time when women were joining the American workforce in increasing numbers, the company endeavored to create an efficient and professional tone in the Home Office. Men and women had separate lunchrooms, and the dress code remained an important part of the office culture.[22]

Barbara Smyth, who started working at Amica as a young woman in February 1943, remembered:

The men had to wear a tie and a suit to work. We didn't have air conditioning back then,

---

Top: In 1947, the company hosted a "Victory Dinner" in honor of employees who served during World War II, as well as to celebrate its anniversary.

Right: Amica's 1947 annual report marks the company's 40 years in business.

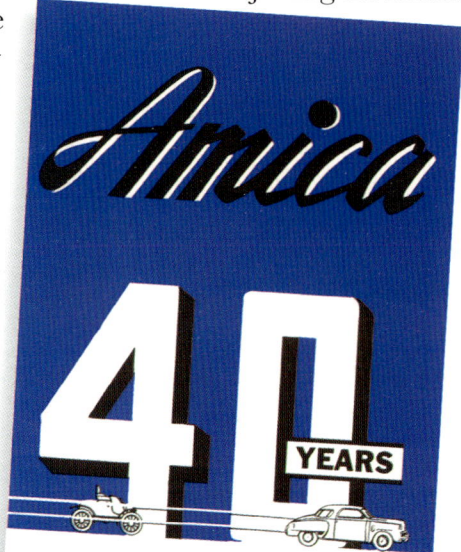

THREE DECADES OF LEADERSHIP

AFTER BEING NAMED president of Automobile Mutual and Factory Mutual in 1940, DeForest W. Abel's commitment to the companies' bedrock belief in customer service was tested. Early in his tenure, when half of the male employees and several female employees were called to serve their country during World War II, Abel accepted no lag in service to policyholders. Throughout the war, the companies maintained an extraordinary record of not asking for a single deferment from military service for any employee.[1]

DeForest W. Abel led Amica for more than 30 years. *(Photo by Fabian Bachrach.)*

Abel led Amica through years of war, including World War II, the Korean War—during which he started the *Amica News* to keep those in the service in touch with their colleagues—and the early stages of the Vietnam War. He also led during economic booms, recessions, and social upheaval with what a colleague would remember as a "tough-minded" management style that was always grounded in an unwavering commitment to customer service and fair claims settlements.[2]

By 1957, Abel had become, in the words of the *Amica News*, "nearly synonymous" with the companies and was guiding them through their greatest period of growth to date. "Mr. Abel," the newsletter noted, "has always been more concerned with maintaining the quality of [the companies'] service, than with increasing our premium income."

Abel served as president of the companies until February 1968, at which time he became chairman of the board and CEO. In 1970, the *Amica News*, honoring Abel on his 80th birthday, stated that "clearly, his wisdom and dignity have been instrumental in securing for Amica the reputation we now enjoy as being the 'best in the business.'"[3]

Abel served as chairman and CEO until February 1971, when he retired from active direction of the companies. During his 31 years at the helm, the companies' assets grew from approximately $17.5 million to more than $167 million.[4] Abel was extolled for fostering the companies' financial strength and culture of integrity.

Perhaps the highest praise of Abel came in the *Amica News* on the occasion of his death in 1977. It stated, "His sincere concern for the policyholders and for the quality of the service provided them, [and] his attention to detail, set a pattern that permeated the entire company and filtered down to every employee."[5]

---

so I imagine they looked for the thinnest suits they could find because it would get warm. Yet, even so, a man always had his coat on.

As for the women, nobody ever wore slacks. You wore a dress or a skirt and blouse. You could wear your slacks when you were off somewhere else, but it was nice to work in a place that was strict like that. Made you feel good. Made you feel that you were important to them, and they wanted you to look right. Women also wore a hat and gloves when coming in to work. A hat and gloves really were a must.[23]

Don Goodby started at Amica in October 1949, two weeks after being married. He joined the underwriting department, which occupied half a floor, working with Albert Pearson, as well as Al Butler,

John Boyce, Bob Thomas, George Burt, and Bill Rice.[24] Goodby also remembered the dress code:

If the humidity and the temperature in those days preceding air conditioning ... exceeded 90 degrees with the windows open, then they would close the office at noontime, and we would go home. ... We used to think [the dress code] was pretty humorous at times, but actually we were proud that the company had the reputation that it had, and that it adhered to its standards.[25]

Amica employees generated respect on the street for their sharp dress and polished appearance. At lunchtime, employees, including Abel, would proceed to the nearby Waldorf Restaurant, where heads would turn as groups of elegantly groomed women and men from Amica entered. The refined style sparked comical confusion among passersby, according to employee Davies Bissett Jr., who said, "If four of us went out to a car to go to a meeting, and people looked at these four people in suits and hats, they would say, 'Oh, there go the police again.'"

This Christmas card from 1946 contained a form that policyholders could use to recommend responsible acquaintances to the company.

At one point during Goodby's early days at Amica, Abel, the company president, addressed all of the employees:

He said that everyone worked hard. He could see the company developing, and at some time in the future, there would be five-figure jobs out there for some of the people in the company. I remember Bill Hunt, a fellow underwriter, said to me on the way out of the meeting, "If [Abel] would change my salary to $10,000 right now, I'd agree to work for that the rest of my career." So it was a whole different outlook. Kind of humorous now to think that anyone in those days would agree to work here forever for $10,000.[26]

The company was flourishing, and employees seemed to enjoy their Amica experience. Abel ran a

WOMEN AT WORK

DURING WORLD WAR II, MILLIONS OF men and women served in the United States' armed forces, but the war also had a profound effect on Americans at home. As historian Brian Metzger wrote: "World War II enabled people to learn about each other and themselves. People of different cultures, backgrounds, ages, and especially genders, experienced massive social changes that would continue in their hearts long after the end of the war."

One of the biggest changes to occur was the perception surrounding the role of women in society. As men left home to serve in the armed forces, and the production of war-related materials intensified, the demand for workers rose. Women, many with children at home, were drawn into the workforce.[1]

As more and more men left to fight in battle, women started assuming traditional male responsibilities. For the first time, women across the country were learning to work as factory workers, journalists, drivers, farmers, mail delivery personnel, garbage collectors, builders, and mechanics. These new opportunities provided women with more independence, which created an increasing sense of empowerment.

Before 1943, as historian Susan Damplo wrote, a lack of childcare options led to high absenteeism among working mothers as the demands of supporting both a family and running a household took their toll. The hostility of many unions and employers to working mothers prompted many women to claim they were childless on their job applications.[2]

This led to the first-ever federally funded childcare programs, which, while terminated after the war ended, would reappear in the 1960s. As the war progressed, a number of states passed legislation to combat salary inequities suffered by women workers, and many unions adopted standards to ensure that female employees received the same salaries as males who performed similar jobs.[3]

While real equality for women in the workplace would progress slowly in the years after the war, its influence on gender roles could not be ignored when the soldiers returned home. In one of the most enduring legacies of World War II, women proved they were capable of equal professional ability and became a permanent element of the modern workplace.

Women became the backbone of the company during World War II, when many male employees were serving in the armed forces.

tight ship, demanding the best from his employees, who, in turn, internalized these high expectations and worked hard to optimize Amica's performance and growth. Phil Lundgren, who started in the transfer department in 1950 for an annual salary of $2,600, described Abel's management style:

> *You made sure that you were there on time in the morning because, when the bell rang, if you were not there on time, you were criticized for that, and they took notes. They had time cards so to speak.*
>
> *Certainly, to begin with, it was Abel Sr. He ruled with—I don't want to say an iron hand—but effectively that way. His word was law. ... If Mr. Abel was going to come downstairs ... whoever was the head of the department, they'd be all steamed up. Make sure that everything was exactly the way it should be and everybody sitting at their desk and paying attention to business. He'd come through with his assistant, Mr. Blair, and they'd look around. They might not say anything, but if there was something wrong, you'd know it later.*

While the company expanded, Amica's values and character remained firmly rooted in company tradition. This dynamic of growth and conservative values created a close-knit bond among Amica employees, as the concept of the "Amica family" was extended to new employees. Lundgren remembered working for Donald Dewing, who was known as Uncle Donald.[27]

There were employee bowling leagues and softball leagues, and the ritual of company Christmas dinners continued. Barbara Smyth remembered that all company events, including the Christmas party, were catered by Laura Carr, a prominent catering firm in Providence. "If you were going to have any catering done, Laura Carr was the one to have, and Amica ... naturally did it the best," she said.[28]

Amica employees worked hard to meet the needs of their customers, and, in return, the company took care of them, as Lundgren explained:

> *I can remember when you had to work late at night, they'd give you $2 in supper money. You would go over to maybe Me Hongs or one of these Chinese restaurants, and you were able to have maybe a beer and still have enough left over for fried rice and whatever you normally would have at a Chinese restaurant: chow mein, chop suey, this type of thing. That would amount to around 90 cents, something like that, and a bottle of beer might be a quarter or 30 cents. You had enough for a 10-cent tip.*[29]

The 1950 annual report celebrated the opening of the San Francisco branch office in 1949, which made Amica a coast-to-coast insurance company.

CHAPTER THREE: FROM COAST TO COAST 45

A program from the annual Christmas party in 1949. Employees remembered that the top-notch catered dinners were among the highlights of the year.

By 1949, the total assets of the Amica companies were approaching $30 million, and, with the opening of a branch office in San Francisco that year, Amica became a coast-to-coast company. The annual report for 1950 featured California on the cover and included some very impressive statistics: On January 1, 1940, Amica had 117,270 policies in force, and by January 1, 1950, it had 202,539 policies, an increase of almost 73 percent. Assets had risen over that same period from $17.5 million to $28.3 million, an increase of 61 percent.

Abel's note to policyholders that year, summing up the 1940s and looking forward to the 1950s, was predictably upbeat:

The record seems good for such a trying period! The events attendant upon World War II made the handling of our business increasingly difficult. First, the manufacture of automobiles was greatly curtailed—then tires and gasoline were rationed— many of our trained men and women entered the armed services and defense industries—well-qualified employees were scarce due to job-freezing orders—and then, when the war was over, there were the many post-war problems to be dealt with. Notwithstanding all these trying conditions, the progress of the Companies has been ever forward!

So now we embark on the next decade with the firm resolve to make an equally good, and, if possible, an even better record.

Abel's optimism would prove well-founded, as Amica would create "an even better record" in the decade to come.

A NEW NAME
For a Familiar Landmark

•

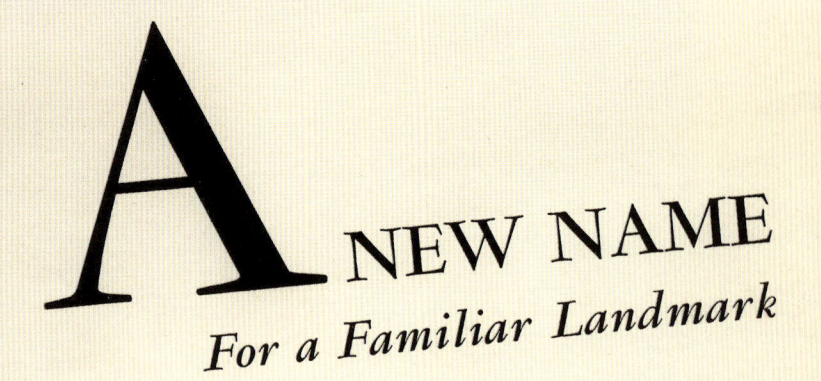

The Grosvenor Building...well-known landmark of downtown Providence...has now been renamed the AMICA BUILDING.

This structure was originally known as the Banigan Building. In subsequent years, its ownership was assumed by the Grosvenor Estate, and the name changed to correspond accordingly.

It was here in 1907 that Automobile Mutual Insurance Company of America was founded in a small one-room office. Here, too, Factory Mutual Liability Insurance Company of America was established in 1921. From these beginnings, the Amica Companies have steadily expanded, until today they occupy much of the building; hence the old landmark takes on the new name, Amica Building.

In 1954, Amica acquired the landmark Grosvenor Building in Providence and renamed it the Amica Building.

CHAPTER FOUR
DYNAMIC GROWTH
1951–1960

My fondest memories are the way we assimilated growth with all the new people coming in. We could just about overcome any circumstance we were confronted with. In those days, doing everything manually, if we had a rate change in a big state like New York, everybody would have to [help]. We worked sometimes late at night. We worked Saturdays. It was real fun getting the job done because everybody pulled together.

—Dave Cassick, Amica retiree[1]

DURING THE 1950s, AS THE FEDeral government built highways and superhighways across the country, the American love affair with the automobile soared to new heights of passion, which in turn meant continued growth for Amica.

Amica continued, in Dave Cassick's turn of phrase, to "blossom."[2] Many veterans, returning from service in Europe or Asia, attended college under the GI Bill in the late 1940s and, by 1950, were ready to join the workforce. Amica hired many new employees, laying the foundation for the company's most dynamic decade of growth yet.

Often, when companies experience the kind of rapid expansion Amica underwent in the postwar boom, the sense of corporate "family" can be diluted. However, any concerns about whether the "Amica Family," so important to the company over the years, would remain intact were quickly laid to rest. The men and women who remained with Amica throughout the war years formed the backbone of the company and helped ensure that the sense of family extended to new employees.

Dave Cassick, who started at Amica in 1949, remembered the rapid expansion of those years as an influx of postwar employees joined Amica, and the company's evolving culture:

It was wonderful. We had only two floors of the building at the time. ... I had been there two weeks,
and new recruits were coming in. I was training people how to write insurance policies after just two weeks because we were on the move. We were just expanding so fast. It was tremendous! Everybody [was] buying a car postwar, and we were the automobile insurance company. We ... just blossomed from then on.

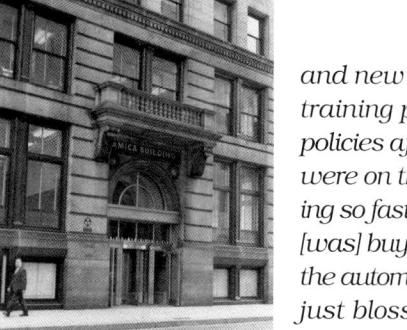

The culture of the company was based on ethics, like it is today. It was the sort of atmosphere where you or I would feel great if we had, for example, a teenage daughter joining the workforce and coming to work at Amica. You'd know it was a quality company and a decent place to work ... because it had personal, ethical rules from DeForest Abel, and he was a very ethical, moral man.[3]

John Boyce, who joined the company in 1950, typified the quiet heroism of so many of the veterans rejoining the workforce. "We all came from different backgrounds, but we all wanted to do a good job in our position," he said. "You have to understand that the economy was really in tough shape when we started, so we obviously all wanted to make a good impression. You kept your head down and did your work."[4]

Over the years, the company grew from one room to occupy much of the Grosvenor Building, later renamed the Amica Building.

The steadfast determination and resolve of returning veterans helped Amica overcome the challenges of assimilating the influx of new arrivals. As the dynamic of Amica's workforce changed, Boyce recalled that women played an important role in facilitating this transition:

> *My generation came in and just flooded the company with the need for more employees as we began to expand, and you sort of looked up to these people [who had been with the company longer]. They were too old to be in the military for World War II, and there were women, too, a lot of women, who just held the companies together. So you sort of looked up to these men and women.*[5]

Harold Hitchen, who started in the stockroom at age 16—a day after graduating from high school in 1951—and would go on to become chief financial officer, also remembered the significance of women employees during the postwar years. "Really, there were all types of people [joining Amica]," he said. "I thought the women were sort of, and probably still are, the backbone of the company as far as getting things done. They knew their jobs cold. It was nice learning from them."[6]

A central aspect that helped bring the "Amica Family" together was the tremendous amount of work that needed to get done and the profound commitment to customer service that went along with it. DeForest Abel, the company's president, reminded new employees of Amica's priority on service. Dave Cassick remembered Abel telling them: "You take care of the customer, and the customer will take care of you." This rallying cry brought the new employees together.

The source of Amica's uncanny ability to retain a strong sense of family and commitment to customer service was best summarized by Carl Hoyer, who joined the companies in 1954: "The people. No question about it. For some strange reason, which nobody can understand or answer, perhaps we have an ability to attract a certain group of people that seem to be dedicated to the proposition of doing a good job and being proud of the work that they do."[7]

Another War Brings a New Way to Stay in Touch

Even as Amica hired dozens of new employees to meet the needs of the post-World War II era, a new conflict arose, and Americans were once again called upon to serve the country. In June 1950, North Korea attacked South Korea, precipitating the Korean War. Many employees were called to their country's service. Some of them, like Gardiner Northup, had previously served in World War II.[8] Yet again, the men and women of Amica served with distinction.[9]

In early 1951, Abel received a letter from Bob Jayne, an employee serving overseas. In it, Jayne suggested that Amica publish a monthly newsletter to be sent to all employees, especially those stationed far from home, keeping them informed of the happenings in the office. In June 1951, the first edition of what would later become the *Amica News* was published, bringing a hint of normalcy to the chaotic lives of those in the service.[10]

Early *Amica Newsletters* included reports about the company—including the announcement of the

DeForest Abel (center) taught the importance of prompt service, saying, "You take care of the customer, and the customer will take care of you."

CHAPTER FOUR: DYNAMIC GROWTH

BRANCHING OUT

JUST AS AMICA ITSELF STARTED MODestly—with two clerks in a small office in Providence, Rhode Island—so, too, did its network of branch offices.

In 1941, DeForest Abel Sr., only recently elected president of Amica, announced a "new corporate strategy for growth with the added advantage of affording better policyholder service."[1] In November of that year, the company opened what became known as "the Boston Office" with one employee.

World War II intervened shortly thereafter, putting the company's expansion plans on hold, but in 1946, the second branch office opened in Springfield, Massachusetts. By 1949, with the opening of an office in San Francisco, Amica could proudly call itself a coast-to-coast company.

In developing a branch office system, Amica faced the challenge of ensuring that its commitment to customer service and fair claims remained unchanged. To that end, Amica dispatched experienced employees from the Home Office to run the new branch locations and to impart the company values to new employees.

The branch office system proved a smashing success. By the mid-1950s, the Amica News reported 24 branch offices in existence and noted that the branches were bringing Amica closer to policyholders. The branches had "become more than company way stations to give the best service; they are emissaries of good will, active parts of community life all over the country."[2] A total of 17 branch offices would be opened during the 1950s alone.

The increase in locations also heightened the importance of the Amica News, which had started in 1951 as a means to keep employees serving in the armed forces in touch with the Home Office. As the company grew, the newsletter began including news of Amica employees spread out around the country, from information about company picnics to birth announcements and promotions.

In 2006, Amica had 38 branch offices throughout the United States, from Portland, Maine, to Seattle, Washington, and from Milwaukee, Wisconsin, to Houston, Texas. These locations have not only upheld the company's values, but have been at the forefront in providing outstanding customer service to policyholders after local catastrophes large and small.

---

impending opening of a new branch office in White Plains, New York—and about activities in Providence. It also provided addresses for employees serving overseas, news of the company softball teams—one of which, the Amica Grays, was leading the league—and a back page titled, "Just Foolishness," which featured lighthearted items like this joke:

> Bobbie—"What are you running for?"
> Jackie—"To stop a fight."
> Bobbie—"Who's fighting?"
> Jackie—"Me and another fellow."[11]

Even the weather was included, depicting the change of seasons and newsworthy occurrences affecting the insurance industry.[12] The July 1951 newsletter noted that a small earthquake had shaken Providence on June 10, while the August 1951 newsletter related that Providence had been hit by a rainstorm and flooding:

> *The streets were curb to curb with water and in low-lying areas the catch basins couldn't begin to take off the surface water so it rose right up over the sidewalks and into the basements of stores and houses alike. The paper said it was the most costly storm we have had since the hurricane of '38!*[13]

In the November/December issue, the newsletter counted 19 employees serving in the armed forces—"three girls and 16 fellows!"—and related that: "The bowling season is under way; 68 men

The *Amica Newsletter* began as a way to keep in touch with employees serving in the Korean War. It included updates from the Home Office, letters from service members, and jokes.

Then Mr. Abel spoke to us, telling something of the wonderful progress made during the year 1951, and of the plans for the future.[15]

Abel's plans for the future included opening a succession of branch offices around the country, and throughout 1952, openings and "contemplated openings" in Raleigh, North Carolina; Seattle, Washington; Los Angeles, California; Salt Lake City, Utah; and Portland, Oregon, were proudly announced in issues of the newsletter.

The newsletter also reported local events that would have been of interest to employees serving in far-off lands. The September/October 1952 edition of the newsletter related an exciting happening in downtown Providence: "On Monday, October 20, Gen. Eisenhower came through Providence on his tour of New England. As is our usual custom, we were permitted to take the necessary time to hear his speech, made from the City Hall steps to an enthusiastic crowd estimated to number 20,000."[16]

The response to the combination of corporate news, employee news, and "foolishness" offered by the newsletters was enthusiastic. Parker Holden, serving in Korea, wrote, "The first edition of the *Amica Newsletter* was most welcome. It constitutes a strong tie for us who are in the armed services with our civilian employer and our fellow employees."[17]

The newsletter proved so popular that in early 1953 the company launched the first edition of the *Amica News*, a magazine-style publication. Under the leadership of Marjorie Chace, the journal featured 12 volunteer reporters at company headquarters and 12 volunteer reporters in branch offices around the country. The expanded publication included sections focused on the Home Office and "Amica Coast to Coast," which included updates from offices around the country, along with announcements of comings and goings, births, marriages, engagements, and transfers.[18]

By the summer 1953 edition of the *Amica News*, Bill Metcalf had taken over as editor, and the publication had grown to include 29 reporters,

competing. 'Russ' Hunt (Underwriting) has the high average of 109%, and he is closely followed by 'Ed' Eaton (Print) with an average of 108¹¹⁄₁₈."[14]

At the holidays, employees were given a colorful and detailed description of one of the company's most important traditions, the Christmas dinner. The January 1952 edition relayed:

By 6:45, we were all seated in the ballroom [at Rhodes on the Pawtuxet] where there were 80 round tables, each laid for 10. The turkey dinner, which was served by Seiler's of Boston, was excellent, and as they are used to handling large crowds (up to 2,500) our group presented no problem. The food was hot, plentiful, and well served.

During the dinner, Tommy Masso's orchestra played and we sang all the old favorites—"Jingle Bells," "Let Me Call You Sweetheart," "I've Been Working on the Railroad," and so on. And after dinner, we all joined in singing two of the traditional Christmas carols.

Dear Friend,

From the day Amica Mutual Insurance Company first opened its doors in Providence, Rhode Island, in 1907, the business has been a true American success story.

As we celebrate this corporate milestone—our centennial year—I hope you will pause to think about the many men and women who came before us. They are the Amica employees whose hard work, loyalty, and enthusiasm provided the mold for the enviable shape of who we are today.

It's my pleasure to share our story—*Amica: A Century of Service 1907-2007*—with each of you, and I want to thank you for the part you play in Amica's ongoing success story.

Others may wonder how a small company with such meager beginnings could become a national leader in customer satisfaction and service, and maybe they will search for the secrets in these pages. But our success story is simple, really. It's all about dedication.

It's about 100 years of genuine commitment from our employees.

It's a story about people at their best.

And it's our story to carry on.

Robert A. DiMuccio
President and Chief Executive Officer
Amica Mutual Insurance Company

two photographers, and—listed separately—two "sports reporters." These reporters wrote articles for the *Amica News* in addition to their regular employment duties.

The section for branch office news included this note:

> *One of our Boston Office claim secretaries was chosen "Queen of the GIs in Korea." The lucky girl was Jane Downey, whose picture appeared in the* Boston Herald Traveler *and was seen by Pfc. Charles Lebow. Greatly infatuated by her beauty, he entered her picture in a contest being run by the Special Service Club, and sure enough, our very amazed but pleased Amica gal won.*[19]

Other highlights of the early *Amica News* included a fall 1953 profile of the company print shop, which each year printed around 300,000 form letters, 2 million envelopes, 400,000 policies, 800,000 office and agents' copies, 500,000 colored blotters, 300,000 endorsements, 1 million circulars and flyers, and 160,000 paperweight calendars. In addition, the shop printed the *Amica News*, Christmas cards, and name tags for parties and outings. The article said the shop was run by "Amica's Ben Franklin—Al Vance. This typographical terror gyrates in a world of his own on the fourth floor of the Home Office Building."[20]

What had started as a way to keep in touch with employees serving overseas very quickly became an integral part of the company culture. As Amica rapidly expanded across the country in the 1950s, the *Amica News* constituted a cohesive element in connecting branch offices and employees together.

Working at Amica

Employees joining Amica in the 1950s found a conservative working environment that valued—as

In 1953, the company began issuing the *Amica News*, a magazine-style publication that featured updates from branch offices, along with news of promotions, marriages, and births.

the company had from the beginning—tradition, teamwork, and superior customer service.

Carl Hoyer described Amica as "a company that did things the right way. There was no question in anyone's mind as to what you should do about something. I found the company to be extremely dedicated to the idea of honesty and fair dealings with all people."[21]

According to many employees, Abel was a strong leader who had a definite vision for the company. He set the tone in dress, attitude, and performance. His excellent reputation in the insurance industry made him a compelling role model for many new and continuing employees.

Priscilla Lowell, who joined Amica in 1954, remembered him as "always so calm, cool, and collected."[22] Abel made an effort to frequently visit the various departments, casually asking employees how their day was going or how their work was coming along.

Before computers became widely available, Amica employees worked with punch cards. Each policy had a corresponding punch card, containing all of the relevant information about the plan and policyholder. For each address change or policy renewal, employees would locate the punch card

The print shop, shown here in 1955, produced an incredible volume of materials, from annual reports to the *Amica News* and invitations to company events.

among a stock of thousands and manually create a new one. Harold Hitchen remembered, "We used to have punch cards, and every premium that was owed to us was put on a punch card. We had three employees who, every time a check came in, would find the appropriate punch card and pull it."[23]

Sultry summer weather sometimes caused difficulties for punch card operators. Lowell related what it was like to work with punch cards in hot weather:

The cards would swell up, and then they wouldn't go through the machine. Then we'd stand hours at a time sorting and getting the stuff analyzed for the statistical part of the program where we had to analyze the city, county, and state, and the rate classes ... and types of coverage that the person had. We tallied all this manually, not by computers.[24]

Dave Bissett Jr. recalled what it was like to work in such a busy office before computers:

I worked at a desk and actually dictated letters. Practically everything was by letter rather than by phone at that time. ... So I would have a stenographer come to my desk, and I would dictate a letter. Then she would go to her desk, type it up, and bring it back. At the end of the day, I might have a stack of letters a foot high to sign.

It was a very labor-intensive atmosphere. Very quick-paced. It took a while to get adjusted to this pace because you would get something in the mail, look at it, and decide what you're going to do about it. Then you'd dictate a letter and, finally, sign it. We were very busy at that time because business was increasing.[25]

Don Goodby remembered one particular source of overtime work, the infamous "Mass Rush":

[W]e worked a lot of overtime in those days because we had what we called the Mass Rush. All the Massachusetts registrations were renewed ... on January 1 each year. So we worked a lot of overtime, maybe staying until 8 or 9 at night, working to renew the Massachusetts policies and getting registrations out so people could register their cars.[26]

The hard work paid off as Amica earned a distinguished reputation with not only the public, but also among its peers in the insurance industry. Bissett said, "It's unusual to have insurance companies who are competitors praise another company, and they did so because obviously Amica had integrity. If we said we were going to do something, we did it."[27] The extensive efforts of employees to fulfill Amica's commitments to policyholders and maintain the reliability of the company would lead to further success as Amica set its sights on further expansion.

Continued Growth and More Challenges

Abel opened the annual report for 1953 with words of caution for policyholders experiencing the new, government-funded "superhighways" for the first time: "Doubtless you are skilled at handling a car at speeds from 25 to 55 miles per hour. But are your judgments and reflex actions fully conditioned by years of driving at considerably higher speeds? Probably not."

He pointed out that too many accidents were caused by drivers who, unfamiliar with high-speed driving, were simply unable to judge how long it took to slow or stop from a running speed of 65 or 70 miles an hour. Abel continued:

When going 70, the penalties of unconditioned reflexes can be terrible indeed, especially when the hypnotic drone of easy mile-after-mile, straight-away speeding dulls the split-second alertness and unerring judgment you need when trouble looms up ahead.

As the nation's transportation infrastructure improved, so did the use of automobiles. In order to satisfy the growing needs of a car-hungry nation, Amica continued to open branch offices. Rodgers Broomhead, who joined the company in 1952 and eventually headed up the San Francisco branch office, confirmed that providing excellent customer service was emphasized in the branch offices every bit as much as in Providence.

Broomhead also remembered how a key company motto came into being. Broomhead recalled a longtime Amica policyholder who turned out to be on the board of directors of a competing insurance company. This policyholder lamented, "I can't very well go around recommending your company. In fact, the people on the board have been asking me why I don't cancel with Amica and go take up the insurance with [the other company]."[28]

Broomhead had responded by saying, "Well, why don't you just tell them that Amica doesn't want to be the biggest? We just want to continue to be the best." When he later told Abel the story, the president enjoyed the sentiment and, before long, Amica was using that slogan.[29]

By the summer of 1958, the company had 24 branch offices spanning the country, as noted in the *Amica News*:

Amica is being brought closer to the insured so that it is not just "a high dividend-paying company back east" to the Westerner, nor a "fast-settling outfit up north" to the Southerner. ... The branches become more than company way stations to give the best service; they are emissaries of good will, active parts of community life all over the country.[30]

Amica's ability to keep down operating expenses was an important aspect of the company's success and enabled it to sustain growth over the years. Yet even as Amica expanded, Mother Nature challenged the companies with a series of terrific storms. In June 1953, a powerful tornado swept through Worcester, Massachusetts, killing 85 people and causing $58 million in property damage. Amica suffered extensive losses, which were paid, as always, "promptly and liberally."[31]

Hurricane Carol hit on August 31, 1954—company payday. John Boyce remembered:

We were always paid in cash, and we were always paid once a month on the last day of the month. ... [T]he accounting people would go over to the bank. They would make up all the paychecks in cash, in envelopes, and bring them back. [On the day of the hurricane], the water started to pile up. By then, we had all been given our month's pay, which was a lot of money.

We had all this cash, and here came the water down the street, while refrigerators started floating down from the Narragansett Electric Company. We were all wondering, "How are we going to get home?" ... We finally decided, "We can't stay here any longer," and we jumped out the first-floor windows, when the water began to recede. Of course, we all got soaked.[32]

Harold Hitchen and Gardiner Northup remembered seeing people in boats out on the swollen Providence River, lassoing the refrigerators that were floating out to sea.[33]

Priscilla Lowell, who received her first pay envelope that day, had planned to go out for lunch with her coworkers, but they were ordered to stay in the building and were eventually evacuated by rowboat later that evening.[34]

Barbara Smyth looked out her sixth-floor office window, saw the water rising, and decided to save her car. She was advised against it but chose to try anyway. As she reached the lobby of the building, the glass revolving door blew in and shattered at her feet. Deciding that discretion was the better part of valor, Smyth went back upstairs.[35]

Phil Lundgren watched as the sign on top of a building across the street toppled and landed on several cars in the street below. The noise of the storm was so intense that Lundgren couldn't hear the crash of the sign.[36]

In the wake of Hurricane Carol, the Amica offices functioned without elevators and power for office machines; they operated by emergency lights and telephone service. Nevertheless, employees were at their posts the next day.[37] Priscilla Lowell recalled, "We had to walk up five flights of stairs for about three or four days before they got any power back, and we worked with flashlights during that hurricane."[38]

Eleven days later, Hurricane Edna hit, and in October, Hurricane Hazel ripped into the mid-Atlantic coast. All in all, the three hurricanes, known as "the terrible trio," accounted for nearly 3,000 losses to the companies. Claims adjusters worked day and night, paying claims at a rate between $50,000 and $100,000 daily. Total payments exceeded $1.4 million within a few short weeks.[39]

Carl Hoyer remembered the lengths to which employees went to keep pace with claims in such difficult working conditions:

I was spending money [on claims] at an absolute phenomenal rate. Back then, we utilized what we called a stated value on the vehicle. So therefore, it was not a matter of getting an appraisal on the vehicle and then maybe negotiating with the owner as to the value of the vehicle. Instead the amount was stated with the policy, and if the value was stated at $3,000, that's what you paid, less the deductible.

So that made it relatively easy, and ... because the mail service was out ... we had a number of [adjusters] brought in from various branches, and not only were we looking at and identifying automobiles and making sure we had the proper car, but we were also hand-delivering checks, which, of course, went a long way in helping the people feel that they were being treated as first-class customers, and that's what they were.[40]

The following year, 1955, brought a fresh batch of storms—Hurricane Connie in August, followed by a severe rainstorm that dumped as much as 16 inches of rain in parts of the Northeast, causing a flood that killed upward of 250 people and caused an estimated $1.5 billion in damage. The West Coast was not immune to the storms, as floods hit from as far north as Washington state down to Southern

CHAPTER FOUR: DYNAMIC GROWTH

California. All of these natural calamities resulted in more and more claims for Amica to pay.[41]

However, the company came through the storms with flying colors. Despite all of the unusual demands on the companies, their combined assets exceeded $50 million for the first time at the close of 1955.[42]

Homeowners Coverage and the 50th Anniversary

By 1956, Abel was convinced that offering homeowners policies would be a sound business decision, and the new operation began on November 14, 1956, under the direction of Don Goodby. Amica's homeowners coverage combined residence fire, personal theft, and comprehensive personal liability insurance in one all-inclusive policy that proved popular with customers.

A few years later, the San Francisco branch again offered service in the finest Amica tradition:

We started tracking our homeowners policyholders on a map, so if they called, we could tell exactly where they were. There was a fire that involved an area where we had a number of policyholders. While the fire was raging, the fire department was trying to put it out and volunteers were also trying to help. We called the people [who] lived on the fringe of that area—not in danger, but could have been in danger—just to let them know that we were watching it, and we would want to hear from them if anything happened.[43]

Above and below: The "terrible trio" of hurricanes that struck the East Coast in the fall of 1954 cost Amica more than $1.4 million in claims. Hurricane Carol was the first to hit. After the storm struck, several Amica employees were rescued from the building by rowboat. Even with the massive losses, the company was determined to pay all claims promptly and fairly, even delivering some checks by hand. *(Photos by* The Providence Journal.*)*

Hurricane *Carol* Lashes Rhode Island

August 31, 1954

Published by
PROVIDENCE JOURNAL COMPANY
Price: $1 a Copy

A Most Important Date

MARCH 1, 1957, WAS, according to the annual report for that year, "a most important date in the histories of the Amica companies." It was a day that marked the 50th anniversary of the founding of the Automobile Mutual Insurance Company of America by A. T. Vigneron in 1907.

The company that started with two clerks working in a small room at 10 Weybosset Street in Providence, Rhode Island, had expanded to include a sister company, the Factory Mutual Liability Insurance Company of America; 900 employees in 22 branch offices across the country; and an increase in assets from just less than $14,000 in 1907 to in excess of $56 million dollars by the end of 1956.[1]

By any standard, the growth of Amica was exceptional, underscoring the effectiveness of the founders' beliefs in providing superior customer service and fair claims settlements. When 1957 arrived, the companies forged ahead under the superb leadership of DeForest Abel, who assumed the role of president in 1940.

The *Amica News* commented on the occasion of the 50th anniversary: "Our president is today guiding us through what may prove to be our greatest period of growth, and he is doing it at a demanding pace and with a force that gives direction to the future."

At the Home Office, the anniversary celebration was understated, focusing on the employees whose service made Amica so successful. Abel himself, well known for his no-nonsense approach to running the companies, walked through the floors of the Home Office distributing $50 bills to every employee.

John Boyce remembered the gratitude the employees felt at the companies' generosity. "That was a lot of money in those days!" he said. "It was wonderful. That was a big occasion."[2]

In his report to policyholders, Abel spoke eloquently about the past and the future:

March 1957 marks the completion of 50 years of service to the insuring public! As we consider the results which have been attained in this 50-year span, we know that the ideas and principles established by the founders were sound, indeed, and that the foundations of the Company were well and carefully laid. From the first, the principle of "Quality" rather than "Quantity" in risks has been carefully observed. As we reach this 50th Anniversary, we feel certain that if the same general underwriting principles and the same conservative management policies continue during the next 50 years, there is no limit to the heights which the company can attain.[3]

Abel's words would prove to be prophetic—though it is unlikely that even he could have foreseen the $3 billion company, with more than 3,000 employees, that Amica is today.

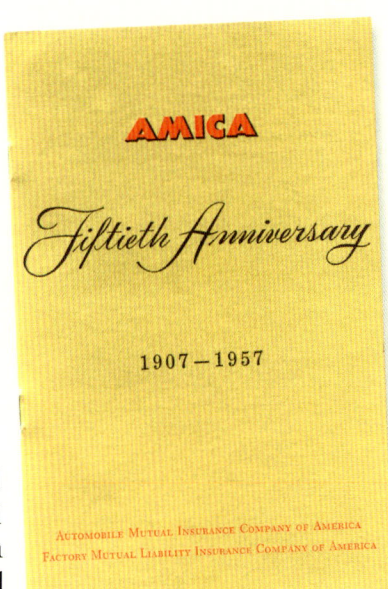

The 1957 annual report commemorated Amica's 50th anniversary, noting that the company had grown to include 23 offices and 900 employees, and was collecting $18 million a year in premiums.

CHAPTER FOUR: DYNAMIC GROWTH

"The Next 50 Years" card sent to policyholders in 1957 looked ahead to 2007, when Amica would celebrate its 100th anniversary.

Abel's cautious approach to new business ventures was validated by the steady success of the new venture. As the 1958 annual report stated, "Of course, only a small amount of business was put on the books that first year, but the calendar year 1957 showed fine progress with premiums in force at December 31 of nearly $150,000. The loss ratio has been very satisfactory."[44]

Abel's consideration for his employees was as great as his business sense. In August 1955, a medical department opened at the Home Office to care for the "many ills that can daily torment the more than 600 men and women employed here." Before long, the medical department was seeing between 25 and 30 people a day. Soon thereafter, Amica began offering health insurance for its employees. According to John Boyce, the incentive for health insurance came when an employee was involved in a serious accident. Boyce said:

Someone in an automobile came down and apparently had a diabetic attack or something. The car went out of control and pinned [the Amica employee] to the building. Up to that time, Amica didn't have any insurance, nor did any company back in the early '50s. Although I must say, if anything happened to anybody, Mr. Abel took care of them. He was a great man.

Well, she was crippled rather badly, but Mr. Abel paid for everything, her medical care and ... the legal resources for her to make a claim against the driver of the car. ... [T]hat was the impetus for the company to put in a formal healthcare insurance plan.[45]

Everyone who worked at Amica in 1957 remembered the day that Abel walked through the office, giving out crisp $50 bills in celebration of the company's 50th anniversary. At a time when bread cost 27 cents a loaf and cigarettes were 22 cents a pack, a $50 bonus was a significant amount of money.

For the rest of the 1950s, Amica would continue to grow, opening branch offices around the country. By the end of the decade, 17 new branch offices had been opened, from White Plains, New York, in 1951, to Phoenix, Arizona, in 1959.

By 1960, as Amica opened yet another branch office—this one in Manchester, New Hampshire—the companies had total admitted assets of $15.3 million and a surplus to policyholders of $12.5 million. A decade of rapid growth was behind the company, and a decade of even more challenges lie ahead.

One of the most significant advances of the 1960s came when Amica began integrating computers into the workplace. A caption in the Spring 1963 issue of the *Amica News* read, "At the Eastern Management Conference in 1963, Mr. Boylan (far right) shows off the IBM 1410 to Mr. Buckless of the Albany Branch Office (left) and Mr. Jamieson of the Rochester Branch Office (center)."

CHAPTER FIVE

DYNAMIC CHALLENGES, CONSISTENT GROWTH
1961–1972

The "Soaring Sixties" became the "Incredible Sixties." Knowledge and technological achievement soared to unprecedented heights. World troubles and despair sank to unprecedented lows.

—DeForest Abel Jr.

AS THE PROSPERITY OF THE 1950s continued into the early 1960s, optimism prevailed in the United States as a whole and at the Amica companies in particular. Now more than a decade removed from World War II and firmly entrenched in the industry and culture of American life, the "Greatest Generation" thrived.

As DeForest W. Abel Jr. would write after becoming president of the Amica companies toward the end of the decade:

We embarked upon the decade of the Sixties with unbounded enthusiasm. The promise of achievements, both social and economic, was great, and nearly everyone believed that the "Soaring Sixties" would lift mankind to a new and higher plane.[1]

Car ownership and the American highway system continued to expand. The annual report for 1964 noted that Americans were "now seeing great highways spreading out over our land like immense tapes measuring the shortest distances between cities."[2] The American population of 188 million owned 82 million vehicles, and the Amica companies were thriving.

In 1962, *Consumer Reports* magazine awarded Amica its highest rating in all three categories as part of its reader survey on insurance companies. Amica excelled at handling first party claims, third party claims, and being least likely to have cancellations and refusals to renew. This marked the beginning of Amica's tradition of earning top ratings from the well-respected publication, a tradition that continues to the present day.

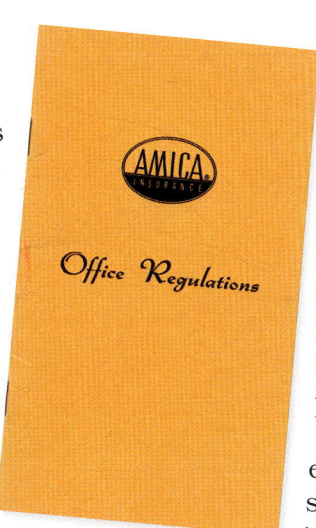

As the Amica companies prospered, employees' spirits remained high, and the sense of family endured, bolstered by pride in Amica's achievements. New employees continued to be at first surprised, then grateful for the conservative office culture, including the dress code, which continued mostly unchanged into the 1960s. Recruits were also impressed with their new colleagues' work ethics, focus on customers, and willingness to share and mentor.

At the 1963 Christmas dinner, employees Barbara Smyth and Jack Hirst sang a song they composed for the occasion. The lyrics read, in part:

*Amica, Amica, Amica
You sponsor this gala occasion*

Company traditions, including the rules outlined in the *Amica Office Regulations* handbook, helped keep Amica centered during the turbulent 1960s and early 1970s.

*A social hour topped with a dinner
That warrants a standing ovation
It gives us a chance to assemble
Apart from our daily employment
To concentrate only on friendship
Combine it with fun and enjoyment
Amica, Amica, Amica
Your 25 year club salutes you
As we gather together this holiday season,
We all say sincerely, "Thank you."*

Only Amica's phenomenal growth surpassed its soaring company spirit. Between 1953 and 1963, the company opened 16 branch offices and increased the number of employees from 658 to 1,030, while its assets grew from about $37 million to $97 million. During the same time, the Amica family also experienced tremendous growth, with 854 employee marriages and the births of 146 baby girls and 172 baby boys.[3]

As business increased for Amica, so did the activity in its mailroom, which was located in the Home Office. As a "direct writing company," written correspondence with policyholders remained a cornerstone of Amica's customer service methodology, making the efficiency of its mailing procedures an important aspect of the business. In 1964, Amica's postage meters recorded 1,686,256 pieces of outgoing mail at a cost of $122,230. In

Amica Song, composed by employees Barbara Smyth and George Hirst, debuted at the 1963 Christmas dinner.

CHAPTER FIVE: DYNAMIC CHALLENGES, CONSISTENT GROWTH

TOP OF THE HEAP

IN APRIL 1962, AUTOMOBILE MUTUAL BEgan a new tradition when it was given the highest possible rating in a *Consumer Reports* reader survey in first party claims, third party claims, and being least likely to have cancellations and refusals to renew.[1] The company received a "better than average" score in all three categories. While employees were justifiably proud of their achievement at the time, they never guessed that they were laying the groundwork for an incredible 40-plus year run of top ratings.

In July 1977, *Consumer Reports* again gave Amica the highest possible rating in all three areas surveyed—handling claims, providing nonclaim service, and being least likely to drop a customer.[2] In September 1984, the magazine switched to ranking insurance companies, and Amica was ranked No. 1 for automobile insurance.[3] The following year the magazine rated homeowners insurance providers, and Amica again ranked No. 1.

That same year, *Consumer Reports* highlighted two factors that contributed to the high rankings: Amica underwriters worked on salary, not commission; and Amica had an unusually high ratio of employees to policyholders, 1-to-140 in an industry in which 1-to-200 was typical.[4]

The trend continued through the 1980s and 1990s, with Amica scoring No. 1 in the *Consumer Reports* surveys for automobile insurance in 1988, 1992, 1995, and 1999, and for homeowners insurance in 1989, 1993, and 1999.[5] In the new century, a massive *Consumer Reports* survey on homeowners insurance conducted between January 2000 and April 2003 placed Amica at No. 1 yet again.[6]

Amica's impressive success in *Consumer Reports* surveys, based on policyholders' interaction with the company, demonstrated that, even as the company expanded exponentially, its commitment to policyholder service has never wavered. Amica never set out to become the largest company, just the best.

addition, many larger envelopes and packages were processed by hand.[4]

In the fall of 1966, Amica marked the 10th anniversary of residence fire insurance and homeowners insurance. At the time, Amica offered coverage in 22 states, "with more to come," and covered nearly $3 billion worth of homes over a 10-year period. Amica's many valuable residences included a home in New Jersey, which Amica insured for $141,000. However, with expensive houses came the possibility of substantial losses, including one "notable loss" in Los Angeles that cost the company $87,000.[5]

On Amica's 60th anniversary in 1967, the company continued to emphasize the importance of customer service:

Every time you communicate with someone, an applicant, an insured, a claimant, a fellow committee man or woman, ... you are involved in public relations. ... This is the impression the public ... has of us.

As Amica continued growing, one of the most substantial changes in its history lay ahead: the advent of computers.

Three Carbon Copies

In the summer of 1959, Andrew Erickson began working at Amica as a part-time employee in the Atlantic underwriting department. At the time, there weren't even any calculators. He recalled:

We had two comptometers in the entire department. I spent a summer doing calculations using a statement pad and a No. 2 pencil. There were no Xerox copiers. The copying process involved about a minute per copy, and it was a very wet, smelly process that ended up with ... white printing on black [paper]. People contacted us primarily through the mail, and use of the telephone was very expensive and discouraged. When we received word from a customer about a car transfer, we sent them a telegram.[6]

Marion Nencka, who started working at Amica in 1960, also recalled the "low-tech" nature of her early days in the Massachusetts underwriting department. Employees sat in rows of wooden desks, and nothing was computerized. Manual typewriters were the norm, and company policy required three carbon copies of all typed material. "Some employees didn't even have telephones on their desks," she said. "The only people who had telephones were the underwriters. ... We actually looked up all the rates in manuals and calculated the actual homeowners and auto premiums on paper."[7]

Computer Revolution

Everything changed after the first sign of the impending technological revolution came in 1963 when Amica rolled out the IBM 1410 Data Processing System for the tabulating department. The machine magnetized a quantity of microscopic dots, called "bits," on a tape one-and-one-half inches wide, 2,400 feet long, and rolled on a reel eight inches in diameter. These "bits" represented the information necessary to print an office copy of a policy. An article in the *Amica News* noted:

Our scientific progress is astounding, and Amica, too, will share in this progress. These magic machines will enable the companies to do a better production job. No one need be concerned about employment. These machines are absolutely necessary to permit the companies to handle the ever-increasing volume of business and the added paperwork involved.[8]

In the spring of 1963, the 1410 Data Processing System began operating as planned. The system, "enclosed in a special air-conditioned room,"

Above and opposite: Photos from the Spring 1963 issue of the *Amica News* showed the company's state-of-the-art IBM 1410 Data Processing System, which was "enclosed in a special air-conditioned room."

looked like a "model kitchen" and gave "an immediate impression of uncluttered efficiency."[9]

Vin McCulloch, who worked as part of the team that converted policies to the computer format, recalled:

We started with New York underwriting, and that was a real challenge, but it was also exciting. I pioneered the concept of word processing with Amica. Much to the surprise of some, word processing was easier.[10]

However, in just four years, the IBM 1410 Data Processing System that seemed so wondrous in 1963 was already out of date, and Amica unveiled a newer and better system. While it once took two to three hours to update endorsements and keep them current on the 1410 system, the new IBM 360 completed the work in just 30 minutes. Even though the 1410 was only four years old, the incredibly fast-paced world of electronics had rendered it relatively obsolete. Now, all of the data regarding a quarter of a million policies could be stored "in line" and was readily available electronically.

The *Amica News* noted: "If the 1410 opened our eyes in wonderment, the 360 almost closes them again in nearly apprehensive expectation of what our next 60 years might bring as Amica utilizes the electronic magic of the space age to bring ever better service to our policyholders."[11]

Computerization gradually spread to the branch offices as well. Peter Goldbecker transferred from the Home Office to Albany in 1972 and found that "there were no computers, only typewriters and some dictating equipment." He considered "the day we received our first green screen computer" a major turning point in the history of Amica. At the time, employees primarily used the first—and only—computer in the entire office for looking up policies.[12]

Employees enthusiastically greeted other modern amenities as well. McCulloch, who worked at the Home Office, recalled two particular conveniences:

> *We removed the old fishbowl lighting fixtures that you now see in old movies and replaced them with ... fluorescent lighting fixtures, and then [several years later] when air-conditioning came, we thought that was the ultimate.*[13]

The advent of computers forever changed Amica's operations, introducing many improvements welcomed by both employees and policyholders. From then on, keeping up-to-date on the latest technology and determining the best ways to implement it became increasingly important.

The "Incredible Sixties"

The soaring optimism at the start of the 1960s suffered a major downturn during the Cuban Missile Crisis in October 1962, which brought the world to the edge of nuclear confrontation. A year later, Lee Harvey Oswald assassinated President John F. Kennedy in Dallas, and what had seemed such a promising time in our nation's history grew clouded with complex issues that bitterly divided the country.

The civil rights movement, the Vietnam War, and the assassinations of Martin Luther King Jr. and Robert F. Kennedy placed an increasing strain on the country even as baby boomers rebelled against the societal boundaries that previously provided such comfort for their parents. As Abel Jr. wrote at the end of the decade:

> *The "Soaring Sixties" became the "Incredible Sixties." Knowledge and technological achievement soared to unprecedented heights. World troubles and despair sank to unprecedented lows. Who could have possibly foreseen that hundreds of cities in the United States were destined to become charred battlegrounds of riots, burning, looting, and killing?*[14]

As the nation struggled with rapid social change, the insurance industry felt its effects as well. Frequent and high claims, expensive court verdicts, and increased costs in almost every aspect of the business plagued the automobile industry during the mid- to late-1960s. Most companies writing automobile insurance barely broke even, while others actually lost money.

The lion's share of complaints about the automobile insurance industry concerned rising premium rates. Across the United States, premiums for private passenger liability insurance increased an average of 23 percent between January 1, 1960, and December 31, 1966. Insurance companies attempted to reduce the impact on drivers by introducing a variety of discounts, yet many people still

---

As Amica spread across the country, the covers of the annual reports spotlighted different states. The 1961 annual report featured Texas and the Alamo.

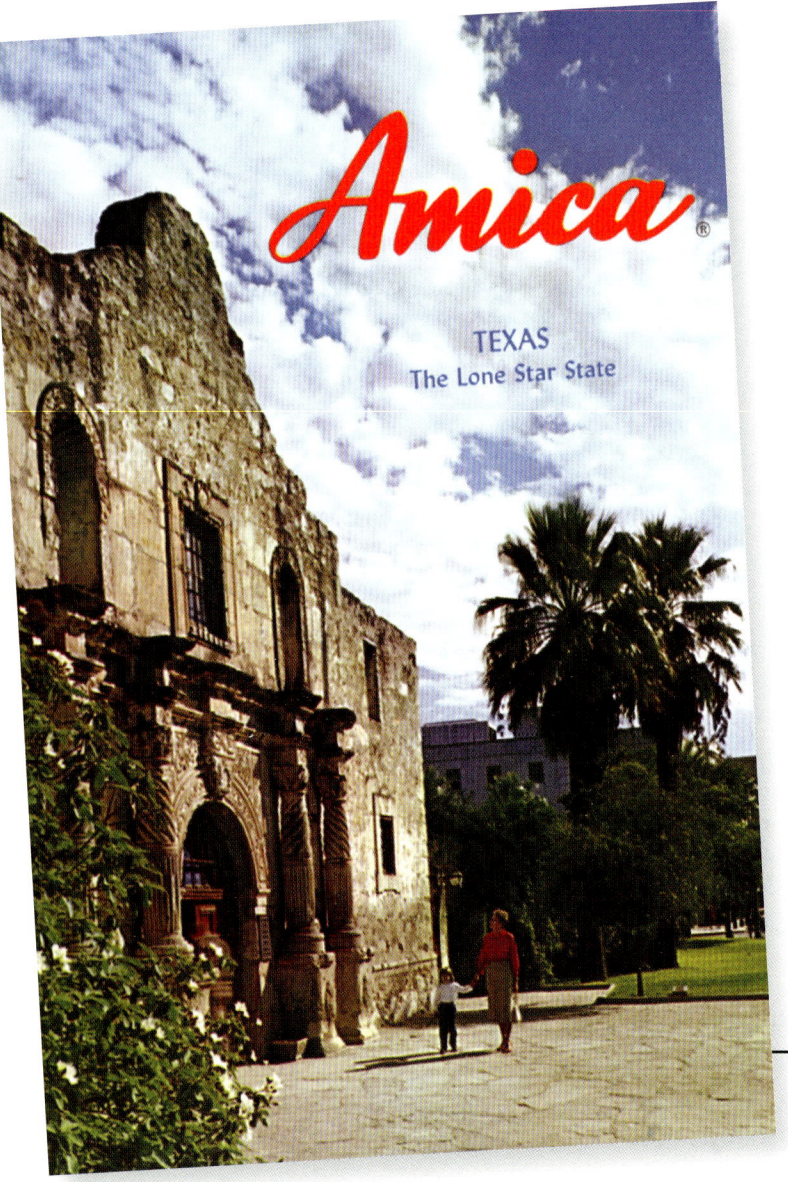

blamed the insurance companies for every attempt to raise prices. However, rates would have increased even more if insurance companies had not absorbed a large percentage of rising costs by losing money on underwriting operations.

As Amica celebrated its 60th anniversary, the 1967 annual report noted that it had returned more than $125 million in dividends to policyholders since 1907. It also pointed out that "inflation of other costs was a major factor in the rise in rates. Between 1956 and 1966, countrywide average costs of medical care rose 39.1 percent; hospital care, 92 percent; [and] auto repair, 21 percent."

Despite public complaints about insurance companies, rates simply reflected inflation and the human and economic cost of accidents on the nation's roads and highways.[15] By the end of the 1960s, an increase in the size and fre-

Miriam Swift was the first woman officer at Amica.

TRADITIONS OFFSET TURMOIL

THE 1960s WOULD PROVE TO BE ONE of the most tumultuous periods the United States had ever seen. The overwhelming confidence and prosperity of the 1950s and the early years of John F. Kennedy's "Camelot" administration ended in 1963 with the assassination of President Kennedy. In the years to come, the country would face racial tensions, a divisive war, and more high-profile assassinations. Meanwhile, social norms changed at an incredible pace.

During the turbulent 1960s, Amica prospered, thanks to its firm foundation in customer service. As the "Message to Our Members" in the 1964 annual report noted: "Efficient insurance service includes many little courtesies and some very important suggestions. It is a pleasant, informative phone call; a prompt, clear reply to a letter; quick response to a claim report; and a competent, satisfactory settlement. It is intelligent recommendations of coverage and personal concern for policyholders' needs. Mostly it is being helpful to clients in a considerate way."

Other long-standing traditions helped the company hold steady during a turbulent decade. Amica continued its commitment to community service, particularly with its involvement in the United Way and the Junior Achievement program. Amica's "regimented" workplace gave employees a real sense of belonging to a special organization. The "Amica Family" was one that worked together, sang the *Amica Song* together at company dinners, and played together on company sports teams.

During an uncertain time, these traditions served to keep Amica on an even keel, moving forward, as it had since 1907, and as it would again in the decades to come.

quency of losses, combined with inflationary operating costs, created an "uncertain economic outlook" for Amica.[16]

In addition to an unpredictable business climate and increasing social unrest, Amica itself experienced substantial change. In February 1968, DeForest Abel Sr., whose steady hand and commitment to customer service had led Amica through years of remarkable growth and unprecedented change, became chairman of the board. His son DeForest Abel Jr. took over as president.

Two years later, in July 1970, Abel Sr.'s 80th birthday was celebrated with a surprise reception.

Left: DeForest Abel Jr. became president of Amica when his father, DeForest Abel Sr., became chairman of the board in February 1968. *(Photo by Roberts Studio.)*

Below: A postcard depicting downtown Providence, Rhode Island, in 1967 shows the Amica Building, second from left.

CHAPTER FIVE: DYNAMIC CHALLENGES, CONSISTENT GROWTH

Accolades included a congratulatory telegram from the governor of Abel Sr.'s native state of Tennessee. An *Amica News* article noted: "Honoring a man of Mr. Abel's stature seems most appropriate at this time. Clearly, his wisdom and dignity have been instrumental in securing for Amica the reputation we now enjoy as being the 'best in the business.'"[17]

Abel Sr. served on the board of directors until his retirement in 1971. During his 31 years of leadership at Amica, assets skyrocketed from approximately $17.5 million to more than $167 million.[18]

Bob Hanke, an Amica employee since 1952, described Abel Sr.:

He had a very strong personality and was ... tough-minded. He had standards that he would not breach under any circumstances. He was a hard boss, but you learned a lot, and he kept the company headed in the right direction. He is the one who really set the tone and philosophy of Amica that still continues to this day.

Above left: Throughout the 1960s, the *Amica News* continued to update the Amica family on company happenings.

Above right: The 1966 annual report featured Oregon.

The new president, Abel Jr., displayed his father's tough-mindedness, and Amica continued to thrive. In a message to policyholders in the 1968 annual report, Abel Jr. noted the difficulties besetting the insurance industry and reassured policyholders that "the operations of our companies ... [are] sound and satisfactory ... [and] in spite of the many problems we face, ... we will continue to strive to do our best for each policyholder."[19]

Above: An Amica wall calendar from 1969.

Right: Amica's Thanksgiving card from 1972. The tradition of sending a Thanksgiving greeting to policyholders has continued uninterrupted to the present day.

In his first "Message to Our Members" as president, he reaffirmed Amica's commitment to customer service:

There has been much discussion of late about the shortcomings of automobile insurance. It is gratifying to learn from our policyholders that our sincere efforts to provide our clients with the best possible insurance protection at the lowest possible cost have not gone unnoticed.[20]

Aside from improving access to services and increasing contact with customers, Abel Jr. expressed his gratitude to policyholders for their continued loyalty and patronage. In 1971, Amica established a long-standing tradition of sending policyholders Thanksgiving cards designed with distinct, original artwork in appreciation of their continued support.

Abel Jr. maintained the conservative culture at Amica that had brought the company family together for so many years. For Ron Bates, a self-described "1960s kid" who joined the Boston Office in 1969, it was initially "a culture shock." However, Bates quickly developed admiration for his colleagues and began to feel comfortable with his coworkers. He felt proud of his job, knowing that, because he worked at Amica, he would not have to compromise his sense of ethics. "In the 1960s, people were suspicious of corporations, [but Amica] seemed very different from what I was led to believe," he said.

Even through changing times and differing fashions, values and professionalism remained Amica's cornerstone. Ken Amylon, who started in 1972, fondly recalled the attitude passed down to recruits by Don Goodby, one of the great company mentors:

Don Goodby, to us, was like Mr. Amica. He absolutely personified Amica's values, and he

always remained determined to do things right. He was a natural leader, and I think any of us would have followed him off a cliff. He bridged the generations. Don ... kept the culture intact.[21]

The famous Amica dress code remained largely unchanged, but Abel Jr. made some minor adjustments, and men were no longer required to wear hats to the office. After the change, Fred Brown, who joined Amica in 1969, remembered going with a colleague to "ceremoniously" pitch their hats in the Providence River.[22]

Other changes were of greater importance. In 1969, Karen Holman, who joined Amica in 1967, remembered:

I think one of the greatest milestones for the company was recognizing that a woman could work, be a mother, and be a member of the community all at once. When I came to work, if you were married and you chose to have a child, that was the end of your work career, and Amica was one of the first companies to recognize the value of adding the opportunity to continue working, instituting maternity leave policies, and allowing women the ability to prove their worth.

I think it is great [that the company recognized] the need for both [parents] to become involved in raising a family. I think that is very special.[23]

Rich McLaughlin remembered feeling the same way after joining Amica in 1971. "The workweek was reasonable," he said. "The demands made upon the time of employees were reasonable. I think it fostered extra time for people, especially people with families, to spend watching their children grow up and participating in more aspects of life than just their job."[24]

The Amica Press was located on Baker Street in Providence.

Confidence Regained

Despite what Abel Jr. referred to as the "winds of change" buffeting the country and the insurance industry in the late 1960s, Amica pressed forward with several new initiatives.[25] The company opened a "bright and spacious new office" in Raleigh, North Carolina, in 1967 and moved in with "no perceptible delay in service to our clients."[26]

In 1969, Amica opened an impressive new printing facility on Baker Street in Providence, Rhode Island. The three-story, 45,000-square-foot structure was "one of the most modern service buildings in the nation" and quickly proved to be a valuable addition, saving time and money while assisting Amica substantially in "achieving its goal of providing the finest possible service to policyholders."[27]

In the summer of 1970, Abel Jr. announced that the new Amica Life Insurance Company, a wholly owned subsidiary, had begun writing life insurance policies in Rhode Island. Philip Lundgren was in charge of day-to-day operations and Joel Tobey served as secretary. Abel Jr. announced:

This is just the beginning. This expansion into the life insurance field provides Amica with the opportunity to offer multiple financial services to its clients in Rhode Island. ... It is expected that Amica Life's operations will expand into neighboring states and become nationwide in scope.[28]

Amica's leadership team in 1968. From left, President DeForest Abel Jr., Chairman and CEO DeForest Abel Sr., and Vice Chairman of the Board Ernest C. Wilks.

CHAPTER FIVE: DYNAMIC CHALLENGES, CONSISTENT GROWTH

The Fall 1969 issue of the *Amica News*. As the turbulent 1960s forever changed society, one thing remained constant—Amica's goal of providing the finest possible service to policyholders.

Despite the rapid changes in society and the insurance industry, Amica continued to focus on its policyholders and employees. In 1970, employee benefits included medical insurance, group life insurance, business travel insurance, and a pension plan.

Taken together, the fringe benefits package represented a substantial addition to employee annual income. While Amica's gross annual payroll totaled approximately $9.6 million, total payments for the benefit plans alone equaled $3.4 million."[29]

At Amica, as in many places across the country, the end of the tumultuous 1960s fostered a desire to look forward with optimism. Typical of this view was an advertisement from a Midwestern newspaper reprinted in the Fall 1970 issue of the *Amica News*:

The news media is constantly pointing out the problems that beset our country, so much so that many Americans may be losing their perspective on what a truly great country we live in. ... Forty-five percent of Americans attend church; book buying has doubled in 10 years; 50 million Americans donate time and 14 billion dollars every year to charity. ... You can add paragraphs of what else is good from your own experience.

The advertisement, as the editors of the *Amica News* pointed out, "makes ... sense to us—perhaps it does to you, too."[30]

As the 1960s ended, Abel Jr. looked ahead with confidence. In the 1970 annual report, he said:

The "Soaring Sixties" became the "Incredible Sixties" and are now safely behind us. It turned out to be a different kind of decade than most of us had expected. While the basic problems confronting our nation, and in fact humanity, remain unsolved, ... we at Amica remain confident as we enter the 1970s because we have prepared for the powerful challenges which lie ahead. Our basic formula for tomorrow will remain the same as it was yesterday, ... providing service to our policyholders.[31]

Another significant change was brewing in the insurance industry with the advent of "no-fault" car insurance. As the 1970s began, Amica planned another move forward—the merging of the two companies into one entity. That merger would propel Amica to even greater prosperity in the years to come.

In October 1976, Amica headquarters grew to include the 23-story skyscraper at 40 Westminster Street (right) as well as the Amica Building at 10 Weybosset Street (left). The $12.5 million addition would give the company ample room for expansion.

CHAPTER SIX

IN UNITY, GROWTH
1973–1984

Now we are one. Effective the first of this year, we became Amica Mutual Insurance Company.

—Amica 1972 annual report[1]

ON JANUARY 7, 1973, A BANNER headline and article in the *Providence Sunday Journal Business Weekly* publicly affirmed that Amica's long-held business principles of customer service and steady, forward-looking growth had helped the companies survive the social and economic turmoil of the previous decade. The headline proclaimed, "New Year Brings New Dimension: Amica Becomes One Firm." It continued:

> Last Monday marked not only the start of a new calendar year, 1973, but the consolidation of two historic Rhode Island insurance companies. Gone from immediate view are the Automobile Mutual Insurance Company of America and its sister firm, the Factory Mutual Liability Insurance Company of America. In their place is Amica Mutual Insurance Company. Thus, Rhode Island is now the home of a company in which total combined assets presently stand at more than $205 million, and in which premiums in force total over $75 million in about a dozen lines of insurance protection. Amica Mutual can point to more than $110 million in surplus to policyholders.[2]

After leading the companies along a path of consistent growth, President DeForest Abel Jr. and the other executives decided that the best way to ensure the strength of both companies was to combine them into one company. On December 14, 1971, Abel Jr. issued a memo to employees announcing the planned consolidation. A lighthearted passage from the 1972 annual report highlighted additional rationale for the decision:

> Our switchboards across the nation had been responding to their calls with "Automobile Mutual," since that was the first of our companies to be established. However, if a person was calling about liability insurance, he would be prompted to ask, "Is this Factory Mutual?"; or if he were interested in financing the purchase of a new car, he would inquire if it were the same as Amica credit. ... Now we are one. Effective the first of this year, we became Amica Mutual Insurance Company. This not only solved the title problem outlined, but effected internal economies and greatly simplified administrative procedures.[3]

An economic slowdown contributed to several difficult years for American companies, and the insurance industry in particular. However, there

Members of the New England underwriting department celebrate the Christmas season by singing carols in 1973.

were also some major improvements to the American economy in 1972. The top financial stories for the year included news that the Dow Jones Industrial Average had reached 1,000 and that the United States had opened trade relations with Russia and mainland China.

The annual report for 1972 declared, "In spite of ... many problems ... the United States achieved an increase in gross national product of nearly 10 percent."[4]

Economic Crunch Continues

Amica faced a difficult financial landscape throughout the rest of the early 1970s. In 1973, the cost of living soared throughout the United States, the stock market plummeted, and interest rates skyrocketed as the prime rate reached a record-breaking 10 percent. Meanwhile, a severe energy crisis caused fuel shortages throughout the United States and significantly affected the entire automobile insurance industry.[5] Amica tackled the problem early on and voluntarily supported conservation measures by cutting back on heat, reducing lighting, and shutting down power to all electrical equipment when not in use. Overall, these conservation measures resulted in a 26 percent cut in fuel consumption in the Home Office and a decrease of 15 percent in the use of electricity.[6]

In the midst of these difficult times, Abel Jr. reminded the Amica family of the values that would help the company persevere:

In the long run, Amica will prosper and stay ahead of the competition only as long as we show personal concern for our policyholders and provide them with the best insurance service at the lowest possible cost.[7]

The property and casualty industry as a whole suffered in 1974, and 1975 would prove even worse.[8] "For our industry, a difficult 1974 became the prelude to a disastrous 1975 as property–casualty insurance companies experienced the largest underwriting losses of their 225-year history," Abel Jr. wrote in the spring of 1976.[9]

Faced with adversity and trying times, Abel Jr. stayed positive, choosing to look ahead to a brighter future. "Our present problems, insoluble

Providence Sunday Journal Business Weekly, January 7, 1973

New Year brings new dimension

'Amica' becomes one firm

Last Monday marked not only the start of a new calendar year, 1973, but the consolidation of two historic Rhode Island insurance companies.

Gone from immediate view are the Automobile Mutual Insurance Company of America and its sister firm, the Factory Mutual Liability Insurance Company of America.

In their place is Amica Mutual Insurance Company.

Thus, Rhode Island now is the home of a company in which total combined gross assets presently stand at more than $205 million and in which premiums in force total over $75 million in about a dozen lines of insurance protection.

And Amica Mutual can point to more than $110 million in surplus to policyholders.

Because of the manner of the consolidation, the charters of the two original firms were amended by the General Assembly to "make and consolidate them" into a corporation by the name of Amica Mutual Insurance Co., "then deemed to be the same corporation as each of the two constituent corporations."

The legislative act also provided that the age of Amica Mutual "shall be deemed to be that of the older of the two constituent corporations" so that Amica Mutual legally is listed as dating back to the founding of Automobile Mutual in 1907 and thereby retains the title of oldest mutual insurer of automobiles in the nation.

The role of jointly-owned subsidiaries—Providence Building Co., Amica Credit Corp., and Amica Life Insurance Co.—is unaffected by the consolidation. All simply become subsidiaries of Amica Mutual.

Nor will the consolidation affect current Automobile Mutual or Factory Mutual policies. These will be honored by Amica Mutual until their expiration, at which time new policies will be issued under the Amica Mutual name.

Historically, Automobile Mutual and Factory Mutual have existed side by side in parallel operation. The separation probably had its roots in the thinking and in the lack of experience in the auto field of more than a half century ago. Nevertheless, the separation has been confusing on more than a few occasions and has resulted in added expense for the Amica families as well.

The consolidation (officials emphasize that it is not a merger) has meant time-consuming, painstaking effort on the part of literally hundreds of people across the country and has involved 50 states, the District of Columbia and the U.S. Internal Revenue Service.

The new name, Amica Mutual Insurance Co., won General Assembly approval last spring and then-Governor Licht signed the bill amending the charters on Rhode Island's Independence Day, May 4. In the following month, the IRS ruled that the move was approved as a "tax-free consolidation."

Additionally, Amica (as the sister companies long have been known) had to obtain approval from the other 49 states and the District of Columbia inasmuch as both firms were licensed to operate in all these areas.

But the greatest challenge lay in the changes which had to be made within Automobile Mutual and Factory Mutual, themselves.

Nearly 3,000 different forms had to be changed—and changed in bulk. These ranged from business cards to letterheads, advertising forms, report sheets and, of course, policies.

In line with the consolidation, too, all signs and door and window lettering either have been redone or are in the process of being changed to conform with the companies' new title.

Officials agree that it will be a year before everything is completely "on stream" but that all the assets of both firms now belong to Amica Mutual and all liabilities have been assigned to it.

What are some of the reasons for the consolidation? In fact, what really were the reasons for the two, parallel companies all of these years?

Ernest C. Wilks, chairman of the board, says that the consolidation was made, above all, to effect certain operating economies and to avoid some confusion.

"Automobile Mutual has been writing automobile fire and theft while Factory Mutual has been writing bodily injury, property damage and collision coverage," Mr. Wilks says. "Now, these are all complimentary lines but in order for a motorist to obtain complete coverage, he had to be insured both by Automobile Mutual and by Factory Mutual."

Also, through the years, each company has had to take out its own license in each state, thus paying double license fees. In addition, tax returns have had to be made by each company in each of the 50 states and in the District of Columbia.

William H. Metcalf, vice president, notes, too, that the change will formalize the name "AMICA" and should overcome any confusion that has grown through the years as the companies began expanding their lines of coverage.

Traditionally, too, under the twin company arrangement, Amica employes have been employed by both firms, simultaneously, and have been paid partially by each. This of course, has meant parallel bookkeeping and other costs for each company.

"We've been thinking about the consolidation concept for several years at least," Mr. Wilks says. "But it was not until December of 1971 that the board of directors decided to go ahead with the plan.

Amica president DeForest W.

CHAPTER SIX: IN UNITY, GROWTH

Still guiding the newly-consolidated firm are Ernest C. Wilks (left), chairman, and DeForest W. Abel Jr., president. As with the Port of Providence, depicted in the mural in the background, Amica has grown and changed through the years.
—*Journal-Bulletin* Photo by EDWARD C. HANSON

Well-known logo will remain unchanged.

as they may now seem, will also be conquered," he said.[10] Even during the worst times, Amica endured, and policyholders' surplus increased by more than $11 million.

As 1975 drew to a close and the recession finally subsided, Abel Jr. noted Amica's resilience and fortitude:

Although the past two years have not been pleasant, Amica has come through this difficult [recession] without experiencing the kind of trauma, in both human and financial terms, that most companies have been forced to live with. For this we can be grateful.[11]

Turning the Corner

The Amica tradition of prosperity and growth continued during the recession. By the summer of 1974, 865 employees worked at the Home Office. The Western and Atlantic underwriting departments, each with 41 employees, moved across the street from 10 Weybosset Street to the "elegant new Hospital Trust Tower, where they occupied the entire 19th floor."[12] To facilitate employee growth, in April 1975, Amica acquired a new 45,000-square-foot office building on 7.4 acres of wooded land in Wellesley, Massachusetts, just outside Boston.[13]

Amica faced even more changes in 1976. On February 2, Amica reached another milestone as it expanded into the marine insurance field. The new protection supplemented Amica's automobile, homeowners, and life insurance policies, enabling the company to service all the insurance needs of its clients in 31 states.

Appropriately enough, the first policy covered a 26-foot Chris-Craft belonging to Len Sweet, the employee initially assigned with underwriting responsibilities for developing and coordinating the new insurance line.[14]

The January 7, 1973, edition of the *Providence Sunday Journal Business Weekly* announced the merger of Automobile Mutual Insurance Company of America and Factory Mutual Liability Insurance Company of America to become Amica Mutual Insurance Company.

In October 1976, Amica occupied the entire Home Office building and an additional floor and a half in the nearby Hospital Trust Tower. To keep up with Amica's phenomenal employee growth, Abel Jr. announced the company had purchased a brand-new, 23-story skyscraper at 40 Westminster Street, next door to the Amica Building. This "dramatic $12.5 million addition to [Amica's] real estate holdings" rose nearly 300 feet above street level and gave the company "a practical way of providing for overflow and flexibility with respect to ... future expansion."[15]

In May 1977, the assigned risk department became the first group of employees to move to the new building. By the summer of that year, Abel Jr. proudly noted that, "Born in one small room staffed by two clerks, [Amica is] now an organization of nearly 1,800 employees operating from 37 offices countrywide."[16]

That year, Abel Jr.'s unwavering optimism about the economic future of Amica and the property–casualty industry as a whole proved justified. "Nineteen seventy-seven was the best year ever for the property–casualty insurance industry, with profits totaling $983 million," he wrote in an article titled, "Turning the Corner" in the *Amica*

Above: A board meeting in session during 1971. Clockwise from left are DeForest W. Abel Sr., Richard M. Field, Clarence H. Rison, Walter E. Mattis, John W. Campbell, Joel N. Tobey, DeForest W. Abel Jr., Robert H. Goff, John W. Blair, Ernest C. Wilks, and Charles M. Dale.

Left: Gertrude Clark accepts a United Way award in 1974 on behalf of Amica employees from Cleo N. Clarke, program coordinator for the John Hope Settlement House in Providence. Bill Metcalf is on the right.

News in the spring of 1978. "Amica's growth in 1977 was substantial. Premiums earned increased 29.3 percent," and company assets reached $253 million.[17]

In November 1978, Amica Life relocated to the recently acquired 40 Westminster Street building, taking over "about one-third of the 14th floor."

Even more important for a company that has always valued customer service over growth, *Consumer Reports* listed Amica as "much better than average" in handling claims, providing non-claim service, and being less likely to drop customers. Amica achieved the highest possible ratings in all three categories of the readers survey.

As Amica celebrated its 70th anniversary in 1977, employees mourned the passing of DeForest Abel Sr. His passion and dedication helped define the company, as the *Amica News* noted:

SKYSCRAPER PUTS MODERN FACE ON AMICA

EVEN DURING THE DIFFICULT RECESSION of the early 1970s, Amica continued to grow. In fact, by 1976, the company occupied the entire Home Office building at 10 Weybosset Street and an additional floor and a half in the nearby Hospital Trust Tower. Amica President DeForest Abel Jr. understood that the company would continue to grow and that even more space would be required to house the company's headquarters.

Since it proved necessary for Amica to have "a practical way of providing for overflow and flexibility with respect to our future expansion," Abel Jr. and the board of directors announced to employees on October 1, 1976, that the company had purchased a brand-new skyscraper located at 40 Westminster Street, next door to 10 Weybosset Street in downtown Providence.[1]

The new 23-story office building, which Abel Jr. referred to as a "dramatic $12.5 million addition to [Amica's] real estate holdings," had been completed in 1971 and rose approximately 300 feet above street level. Amica honored the leases of all 40 of the building's tenants, and in May 1977, Amica's assigned risk department became the first group to move into the new building.[2]

The new skyscraper remained Amica's home for almost 20 years, until the company moved to its current location in Lincoln, Rhode Island.

The penthouse atop the Amica Building at 10 Weybosset Street (center foreground) adds a new dimension to the Providence, Rhode Island, skyline as renovations to the Home Office building continued in the early 1980s.

[He] led Amica for 31 years. His sincere concern for the policyholders, for the quality of the service provided them, [and] his attention to detail, set a pattern that permeated the entire company and filtered down to every employee.[18]

Retaining the Amica Culture

Throughout its history, Amica met the challenge of incorporating new branch offices and employees into the company without sacrificing its commitment to customers and while retaining a sense of family.

Paul Pyne, who joined Amica in 1977, recalled how even the look of the Home Office bespoke tradition:

There was just an impression that you had when you went into the old Home Office. It was like stepping back in time. They had oak wood partitions, and the bottom of the partitions were oak wood with glass that separated the different office cubicles. [It looked] like a company that [had] tradition and had been there ... for quite some time.[19]

Bruce Maynard joined Amica in 1977 and realized almost immediately the value of Amica's unique culture. He explained:

You learned early on that Amica had a strong focus on quality in everything that was done. There

Left: Schwartz' rendering of the building Amica acquired at 40 Westminster Street is based on an architectural model by Shreve Lamb & Harmon Associates Architects in conjunction with Associate Architect Ira Rakatansky.

Below: Workers prepare office space on the sixth floor of the new building two months before moving day.

Above left: Tennis was one of many extracurricular activities encouraged by Amica. From left are Fran Bisignano, Stephen Kane, Sandra Cook, and Jack Anderson.

Above right: From left to right, Sandy Fratantuono, coach Carl Potter, and Fran Bisignano show off trophies belonging to Amica's women's softball team, which won the State Women's Industrial Softball Championship for the third consecutive year in 1973.

was one way to do things, and it was clear and simple; you did things the best way possible. It was clear to me that there was a genuine feeling of pride associated with working at Amica and that was a result of the company's commitment to its customers and employees.[20]

The kindness of Amica employees reflected the company's devotion to customer service. Happy, well-treated employees made for happy, well-treated customers.

Melburne McLendon first heard of Amica in 1950 as a young lawyer practicing law in Atlanta. He recalled:

Amica did not operate like other insurance companies, which frequently sought the cheapest way out of a settlement with their insureds. Instead, Amica tried to find a way to support the policyholder's claim and take whatever action was necessary to bring all claims ... to an immediate and satisfactory conclusion. We clearly understood that there should be no dragging of feet in disposing of a claim. That was ingrained in me 50 years ago.[21]

Amica ensured its core values extended into its branch offices by extensively training employees at the Home Office before transferring them to a branch. Ted Murphy, who joined Amica in 1980, trained for six weeks at company headquarters before being assigned to the Cleveland Office. Murphy said his training stressed certain ironclad tenets of Amica's philosophy. "The customer is king," he recalled. "The customer is always right. Those types of things that actually seemed clichéd, Amica actually believed and lived by, and we were expected to do the same."[22]

Murphy fondly remembered the differences between Amica adjusters and adjusters from other companies. "Our caseload was never as overwhelming as those of other companies," Murphy said. "[For them,] it was all about how many cases they closed. With us, it was about covering all the bases on a claim. Maybe that's not the most efficient [way to do things], but it's certainly what has gained us our reputation of being the best in the industry in terms of service."[23]

Pyne also recalled that, while working as an adjuster for other companies could be difficult, working at Amica was "a pleasure" because Amica adjusters focused on serving the customer. "It's the integrity of this company that really comes into play

Above: In 1974, Amica celebrated 25 years of commitment and service to Junior Achievement.

Right: Both men's and women's softball teams were good-natured and competitive. Pictured here, Coach Bob Phayre, wearing a jacket, and his team enjoy a big inning at a game in 1974.

at this point, because we stand behind our product," he explained.[24]

The Amica family thrived because of the high standards of the company as well as the rich traditions of extracurricular activities and community service. Amica supported men's and women's softball teams, as well as a bowling league, and remained extremely active in community service programs such as Junior Achievement and the United Way.

In 1974, on the 25th anniversary of Amica's commitment to Junior Achievement, Abel Jr. noted:

Amica's record as a concerned corporate citizen is a long and distinguished one. Among the many worthwhile causes we have supported through the years, our quarter-century commitment to Junior Achievement stands as a unique accomplishment.[25]

In 1976, 95.5 percent of all Amica employees at the Home Office participated in a United Way fund drive, earning the company a United Way Award for Excellence.[26] These activities provided Amica employees with opportunities to enjoy each other's company and take an active role in their community.

The Blizzard of 1978

On Monday, February 6, 1978, forecasts predicted snow flurries, but as morning turned to afternoon and the sky remained overcast, many employees at the Home Office assumed that the predicted snow would not materialize or would amount to only a few inches. Word soon began to spread of a blizzard heading toward Providence, however, and many businesses closed down.

Shortly after noon, the skies unleashed one of the worst blizzards in Providence history. When the snowfall finally ceased, 27 inches inundated the city streets, effectively shutting down the city and prompting President Jimmy Carter to declare portions of Rhode Island a federal disaster area.

At 2:00 P.M. on the day of the blizzard, with the snow already "heavy and blowing hard," Amica closed the Home Office so that employees could avoid the worst of the weather and traffic and return home safely.[27]

John Boyce was one of the last to make it out of the city that day. He recalled:

We left at about two o'clock in the afternoon. The snow was coming down like crazy, and I think I was the last one out of Providence. Because of the front wheel drive on my Volkswagen, I was able to

BLIZZARD'S IMPACT WIDESPREAD

WHILE THE EFFECTS OF THE BLIZZARD of 1978 were felt strongly in Providence, the storm's impact reached far beyond the city. On February 6, the day of the blizzard, Massachusetts was still recovering from a record snowfall in Boston on January 20, where more than 25 inches fell.

Some forecasters had predicted only six inches of snow the day the blizzard hit, but by the time it ended, Boston received more than 27 inches and remained mostly closed down for the week.[1] Winds gusted to hurricane strength, and tides rose drastically.

On Route 128, the main highway outside Boston, more than 3,000 cars and 500 trucks were stranded by the storm. Ninety-nine people in Massachusetts lost their lives, and thousands of homes and businesses were destroyed or severely damaged, which in today's economy would have resulted in approximately $2.3 billion in damage.[2]

In Rhode Island, 26 people died, and property loss was extensive. President Jimmy Carter declared portions of Rhode Island and Massachusetts federal disaster areas, and the National Guard assisted in recovery efforts.

With Providence still closed to private vehicles after the Blizzard of 1978, Jack Durnin and Fred Gifford, in hats on the far right, scout the best path to the Home Office, a block away. *(Photo by The Providence Journal.)*

go up on sidewalks to get around cars that were stuck. I think I was the last one to get up the hill [past the Washington Bridge]. I made it as far as my driveway, but it was buried in snow. I found out several days later [that my secretary] made it as far as Route 146 and spent the night in a church basement, along with other people trying to get home.[28]

Other employees, however, did not leave soon enough, and many remained stranded in the office. Don Goodby attempted the trek home, but didn't get very far that Monday afternoon. "[I made it] about half a block and saw that everything was stopped solid," he recalled. "I pulled back into the company lot and went back into the office."

He slept in his suit and topcoat on the floor of his office that night and every night that week before finally making it home on Friday. Goodby also recalled that Ernie Wilks, Amica's chairman of the board at the time, left the office that afternoon, but only made it as far as the Providence Marriott. He pitched in as a kitchen worker for days until he could make it the rest of the way home to Woonsocket, Rhode Island.[29]

Goodby was one of about 50 "refugees" stranded in the Amica building that week, including more than a dozen people who did not work for Amica but were marooned in their cars or left waiting for city buses that never arrived.[30]

President DeForest Abel Jr., a refugee himself, gathered the rest of the staff and immediately went to work feeding and caring for the stranded guests, making them as comfortable as possible with limited resources.

Guests slept on the floor, and the diet generally consisted of sandwiches. During the first few days after the blizzard, food was scarce, since most downtown restaurants remained closed. According to the *Amica News*, "Mr. Abel and many others hiked through the snow to nearby stores and clubs to obtain sufficient food to feed everyone."[31]

The staff did more than just care for the people at the office. They remained determined to keep the phone lines open so that distressed policyholders could receive company assistance.

Every day that week, with the city of Providence essentially shut down, Amica employees staffed the phones and provided as much service as possible to branch offices and policyholders.[32]

Dave Cassick actually made it home the day of the blizzard, but he decided to return to the office to help out. He remembered working every day for at least five or six hours until the office officially reopened a week later. Others, including volunteers, worked on claims and ensured that all vital operations continued.

While the Great Blizzard essentially shut down the entire state of Rhode Island for a week, according to the *Amica News* it "proved to be ... another opportunity to demonstrate those qualities that have made our company unique in the industry."[33]

Computers Take Over

As the 1970s gave way to the 1980s, the progress of technology remained constant at Amica, and computers steadily took over the workplace. Leading the way were employees Dick Leonard and Norm Bell. According to Lou Peranzi, who joined the company in 1974, it was their leadership that guided the transition from tabulating to true information technology.

Jim Devine started working as a computer programmer trainee at Amica in 1973 and would go on to become senior vice president of corporate information systems. He vividly remembered the state of technology during the early 1970s and the laborious process of programming the computers, as well as the large space required to house the massive machines. He recalled:

We were using mainframe computers that would take up half a floor of our building and had only a fraction of the computer processing power that we now have on everybody's desk in their PC. The mainframe computers were slower, with less storage and less memory than a ... desktop computer today.

Disk drives back then were the size of a household washing machine or a dishwasher, and they had large platters of disks on them. We would have a whole room full of them. Now thousands of times the amount of storage is in a machine the size of one washing machine. It is amazing how much the technology has changed.[34]

Devine said that Amica was determined to stay ahead of other companies when it came to adopting new technology. "Some industries were more geared toward new technology, but I think in the insurance industry we were at the forefront with some of our systems," he said.[35]

Lou Peranzi, who succeeded Jim Devine as senior vice president of corporate information systems, played a key role in Amica's transition to a computer-based workplace. When he started, only 22 to 23 employees worked in the data processing department, now known as corporate information systems. By the end of the 20th century, that figure would balloon to more than 300.

Aside from their enormous size and lack of storage capacity, the computers also posed other problems. To ensure that the machines did not overheat, Amica spent tens of thousands of dollars on chillers to cool them. Though the machines were no better than today's small desktop computers, they provided great advantages. Peranzi recalled:

In the late 1970s, we started to put our first transactions online. Prior to this, when someone would call on the telephone and they wanted to purchase insurance, we would have a form that someone would take, and they would write all the information on it and then go back and type it. Then they would notify the accounting department that we had to present a bill to this person. Then they would take that file, that policy, and they would file it away.

The filing system was very elaborate, but it would be in a file drawer. If customers called back because they wanted to change their policy, had a question about their policy, or had a claim, [someone] would have to go and pull that paper file up,

Attendees at the 1981 Christmas dinner sing along with the after-dinner entertainment.

see what they were insured for. Everything was very paper-driven and very archaic.[36]

Meredith Taylor, who joined Amica in 1977, vividly remembered the filing cabinets. "We manually typed policies," she recalled. "There was just no end to the filing cabinets and the piles of paper and the lists of jobs."[37]

Kathleen Curran, who would go on to become vice president in rating information services, joined the company in December 1979. At the time, the department consisted of only four people, and all calculations were done manually. "We did have limited access to the mainframe computer, but most of the work consisted of crunching numbers on a calculator," she recalled. "It was certainly different from using spreadsheets today."[38]

John Connors remembered the arrival of "green screen" computers, an important step in the progress toward company-wide computerization. Eventually, employees received their own personal computers. "It turned out to be very important for Amica in two ways," Connors said. "It vastly improved the quality of the service we were able to deliver, and we were able then to have changes in the mail to people in a matter of days instead of weeks. Both the quality of our service and our efficiency improved dramatically."[39]

Wendy Sturn, who joined Amica Life in 1981, recalled the transition:

DeForest Abel Jr., left, and Bill Metcalf were among many employees who participated in Amica's blood bank program on July 13, 1984.

Handwriting everything and ... having to research whether these policyholders had other coverage with Amica was very time-consuming. Then the computer system came in, and we thought we had gone to heaven because everything was at our fingertips. With just a couple of clicks, we could find out if our policyholders had auto coverage, homeowners coverage, and where they lived or if they had dependents.[40]

Telephone technology also changed rapidly. Meeting the fast pace of business required maintaining a competitive edge to keep Amica's service the best in the business. The company installed new communications equipment in the Home Office in August 1980, which included more than 500 advanced telephones in the Providence buildings. The new phone system featured the ability to transfer calls, answer a remote ringing telephone, provide automatic callbacks, and establish a three-way conversation "within our building or between parties thousands of miles away."[41]

Since customer service remained of paramount importance, all new technologies were valued for both efficiency and improving Amica's service to its customers. In 1984, in an additional advancement in customer service, Amica adopted another innovative telephone technology—the 800 number. Amica's new 800 number, 1-800-24-Amica, connected customers to the nearest branch office.

Savings, Growth, and a Change at the Helm

In 1980, the company introduced the Amica Savings Plan for employees, which proved to be a very popular benefit. It continues to provide employees with an easy way to save a portion of their salaries through payroll deductions with a company match on the first 6 percent saved and important tax advantages.

During the early 1980s, Amica experienced rapid growth. On the company's 75th anniversary in 1982, Abel Jr. observed that Amica reported "its 75th consecutive year of growth," despite a "roller coaster year" in which "the economy sagged [and] stocks soared" while a recession hit America. Meanwhile, the property and casualty insurance business as a whole recorded $10.4 billion in losses.[42]

In its first 75 years, Amica grew into a company employing 2,300 people in 38 offices nationwide. The company's earned premiums grew from $11,000 to $230 million, its assets rose from $14,000 to $446 million, and its surplus skyrocketed from $1,488 to $170 million.[43]

Amica also began offering personal umbrella liability insurance in 1982. Despite a "revolution in insurance," during which industry giants branched out into other financial services, Abel Jr. reiterated in his annual report that Amica would continue to focus on its core business, in contrast with "mega-organizations that try to be all things to all people."[44]

Three years later, Abel Jr. retired after 34 successful years with the company. On January 1, 1985, Amica executives bid farewell to the man who helped the company prosper despite social turmoil, economic recession, and other hardships. The *Amica News* noted:

Throughout his long career, Mr. Abel has seen Amica evolve into one of the best insurance companies in America. We thank him for his part in our growth and prosperity and wish him well in the years ahead.[45]

Following Abel Jr.'s retirement, Executive Vice President and Secretary Joel N. Tobey took over as Amica's new president and CEO.

From the time it began in one room at 10 Weybosset Street in Providence, Rhode Island, in 1907, to its move during the 1990s to the suburban Lincoln Center Office Park, Amica has refused to waver from its mission of providing the best customer service in the industry.

CHAPTER SEVEN

JUST THE BEST

1985–1995

We have never wished to grow just for the sake of growth. Our historic emphasis has been on policyholder service. We don't seek to be the biggest, just the best.

—Joel N. Tobey, former Amica president

EVEN DURING THE SERIES OF recessions that beset the nation during the 1970s and early 1980s, Amica continued to thrive. In fact, 1984 was the company's most successful year to date.[1] It was "a year of change for Amica, one that proved the 'sturdiness' of the company once again," and ended with "perhaps the most significant change of the year" when company president DeForest Abel Jr. retired and Joel N. Tobey took over as president on January 1, 1985.[2]

Before joining Amica as an underwriter in 1960, Tobey graduated from Brown University and served for eight years as an officer in the Army's airborne infantry. In 1965, he moved to the newly opened Baltimore Office, where he soon became assistant branch manager. He remained in Baltimore until 1967, when he returned to the Home Office as an assistant secretary, his first senior management position. He began serving as secretary of the Amica companies in 1968, and received a promotion to vice president and secretary in 1972. After being elected to the board of directors in 1975, he was appointed executive vice president and secretary in 1980.[3]

Upon becoming president, Tobey emphasized the qualities that made Amica the best in the business. In the annual report for 1984, in an article outlining "the expectations of our new president," he wrote:

Amica's belief in considerate, efficient service and sound underwriting has brought steady growth and prosperity for the past eight decades. However, the years ahead promise to be particularly challenging. The insurance industry is presently being swept by changes that could significantly alter the current system.

Advances in technology have allowed for the creation of sophisticated financial networks offering everything from securities investments to IRAs and traditional insurance coverages. As a result, competition has become intense as companies inside and outside the insurance industry scramble for a larger share of the financial services market.

Coping with this increasingly crowded and competitive environment will be a matter of foremost concern to Amica's new management team. As we prepare our goals for future corporate growth, we are confident we will succeed, for we will be relying upon our greatest asset—our dedicated staff of career employees from coast to coast.[4]

In "A Message from the President," Tobey pointed out that "change is absolutely necessary for any

---

Joel N. Tobey became president of Amica on January 1, 1985, when DeForest Abel Jr. retired.

healthy, growing company, and we feel confident that Amica has come through 1984 better and stronger than ever ... and we can all be proud of that."

As president, he vowed Amica would not become complacent, nor would it "rest on the laurels of ... past successes."[5]

In 1985, as Amica approached its 80th anniversary, the company published a narrative history that provided an excellent overview of the changes and growth Amica had undergone since its founding. It read, in part:

We, the Amica companies, have grown ... [since] the days when a handful of staff members could shoulder all of the work to a company of 2,200 people, about half of us in the Home Office and half in the field. [We have grown] from a single room in the building at 10 Weybosset Street, to ownership of the entire building, to acquisition and gradual occupation of the building next door at 40 Westminster Street, to 39 branch offices around the country. We used to type all of our correspondence manually. Today, we continue to provide prompt, personal service to our growing number of policyholders with the aid of high-speed electronic computers and word processors. ... Today our financial position is one of the soundest in the industry, with assets approaching $700 million dollars. We consistently receive the highest company ratings. We have grown a bit, but our operating philosophy has not changed. Each of us still strives to provide the best, most personal service possible, and most often we exceed.[6]

Tobey and the rest of the company understood that Amica employees always were, and would always be, the driving force behind the company's success. Traditionally, Amica boasted high employee retention rates and frequently highlighted the service and loyalty of long-standing employees.[7] New Amica employees learned of the company tradition of providing exceptional customer service starting from their first day on the job.

David Kenny, who joined Amica in 1985, remembers his first impression of Amica as a "conservative" company that "had its act together" and was a good "corporate citizen that cared as much about its insureds as it did its own employees." He recalled the pleasant work environment at Amica:

There ... is a positive atmosphere of enthusiasm among the employees. Having worked for the company in different geographic regions, I've made some good friends in those offices, and when I've moved to another office, it's been almost like leaving family.[8]

Jim Will, a recent college graduate in 1986, interviewed with Earl Minerd, a 20-year Amica employee, for an adjuster position. Just prior to his interview at Amica, Will worked briefly for another insurance company "that made many promises but did not deliver."

Will found the company's culture intriguing because of the way Amica treated employees and pol-

Joel N. Tobey reinforced Amica's commitment to its core values with a new Statement of Corporate Mission.

Members of the Worcester claims staff in 1987.

icyholders. Whereas his former employer was simply concerned about sales, Amica focused on prompt service and customer satisfaction. He explained:

> *We want to pay what we owe as soon as we can. I think that's definitely true whether it is a first-party claim or a third-party claim. I think claimants quickly realize that. If they are listening and they are rational, they quickly understand that we are not there to try to take advantage of them. It is still intriguing to me that Amica can be so successful in this industry without a large sales force out there pushing the product.*[9]

Founding Principles in Action

Amica's commitment to serving its policyholders helped the company build a loyal base of customers. In 1985, Amica had 60,000 insureds who were with the company for 25 years. Of those, 5,000 were with the company for more than 50 years, and three had first joined the company in 1915. Policyholders recommended Amica to 11,000 new customers in 1985.

Tobey reaffirmed the company's commitment to its core values and summarized the company's values and principles in a Statement of Corporate Mission. In 1985, Amica sent letters of recognition to 5,000 policyholders insured with the company for 50 years or more.[10] The letter stated that Amica was "most grateful for your loyalty, and [we] want you to know how much we value your support and friendship."[11] Over the coming months, the letter prompted more than 300 cards, letters, and phone calls from appreciative policyholders around the country.[12]

Upholding Amica's Vision

JOEL N. TOBEY, THE NEW PRESIDENT of Amica, understood that Amica's great success over the years was rooted in fulfilling its commitments to policyholders and employees alike, and set out to put Amica's values in writing. The result, a Statement of Corporate Mission, was unveiled in December 1986. It read:

> Amica's corporate mission is to provide the best personal insurance protection for individuals and their families at the lowest reasonable cost, consistent with sound financial management. In accomplishing Amica's mission, we will be guided by the following:
>
> 1. Our operating philosophy is to achieve profitable growth by writing only exceptionally good business.
>
> 2. Our tradition of excellence in addressing client concerns sets us apart from other insurance companies and will not be compromised.
>
> 3. We value the unique dedication and professionalism of our employees countrywide and are committed to providing a pleasant, safe work environment with equal opportunity for personal growth and recognition.
>
> 4. We adhere to the highest ethical, moral, and legal standards in our business and civic activities.
>
> 5. Amica seeks not to be the biggest, just the best.

Tobey saluted Amica's policyholders in the 1985 annual report, personally thanking four of Amica's nearly 400,000 families. "[They] have discovered [our commitment to service] for themselves," he wrote. "Through them we pay tribute to each of you. Our success is measured by your satisfaction."[13]

The Vranizans of Oregon were one of the families profiled. The report noted:

> Catherine Vranizan, at 82 years old, is the oldest of the Amica-insured Vranizans. Her three sons Matthew, Edward, and Ralph, as well as her nephew Jim Vranizan, make up the second generation. Third-generation policyholders include Jim's son, Richard; Matt's son, Peter; Ralph's daughter, Helena; and Edward's two daughters. ... Jim was the first to insure with Amica. He and his wife ... insured their car with Amica in 1957 and added their home in 1961.[14]

As the Vranizan family's story clearly confirmed: "The Amica tradition for service was not only recognized and heralded by various journals and consumer organizations, but has been made meaningfully evident by the widespread extension of our services to the sons and daughters of earlier insureds."[15]

By 1986, Amica ranked as the seventh-largest mutual property and casualty insurance company in the country, but did not come close to the size of the multibillion-dollar industry giants. And that is just the way Amica liked it:

> We have never wished to grow just for the sake of growth. Our historic emphasis has been on policyholder service. We don't seek to be the biggest, just the best. ... We were particularly privileged to be singled out in the February 2, 1987, issue of Time magazine as a company that lavishes care on its customers. To receive national recognition for something in which we believe strongly is very gratifying. It is a tribute to all Amica employees, past and present.[16]

That year, the Amica Life Insurance Company thrived. The staff grew to 119, the company became licensed in 46 states, insurance in force totaled more than $2 billion, and the company again received an

"A" rating from A.M. Best, the leading insurance reporting organization.[17]

Throughout its 80-year history, Amica weathered wars, depressions, recessions, hurricanes, and earthquakes. Nineteen eighty-seven was no different, as the company faced major challenges, including a major stock market crash and implementation of the 1986 Tax Reform Act. In the 1987 annual report, Tobey wrote:

Once again, we have had a good year in spite of all odds. Our surplus to policyholders and total assets were over $311 million and $999 million, respectively, at year-end.

An Amica insurance policy is not a commodity. Our financial base is your guarantee of protection through good times and bad. And although we continue to seek profitable growth, we refuse to do it at the expense of our commitment to quality service.[18]

In 1988, Amica's year-end assets exceeded $1 billion for the first time. "Another positive event for Amica was its inclusion in a new book [titled] *The Service Edge*," according to the 1988 annual report. "Authors Ron Zemke and Dick Schaaf singled out 101 companies countrywide that excelled in service 'because of their belief that they can approach perfection if they just keep at it.'"[19]

The Service Edge also pointed out that Amica achieved "Satisfaction Index" scores of 91 out of 100 from *Consumer Reports* magazine in 1984 for car insurance and in 1985 for homeowners insurance. While Amica was the seventh-largest mutual property and casualty insurance company in the United States, it remained "more interested in being the best, even if that means it can never be the biggest."[20]

Opportunities for Service

Amica has a long-standing policy of responding to catastrophes as quickly as possible. Stuart Towsey, who joined Amica in 1973, explained:

One of the first things we do is ... contact our insured and provide the best service possible. Our claims department makes sure that we have adequate people there to answer the phones. If we need outside adjusters, we fly them in. We have

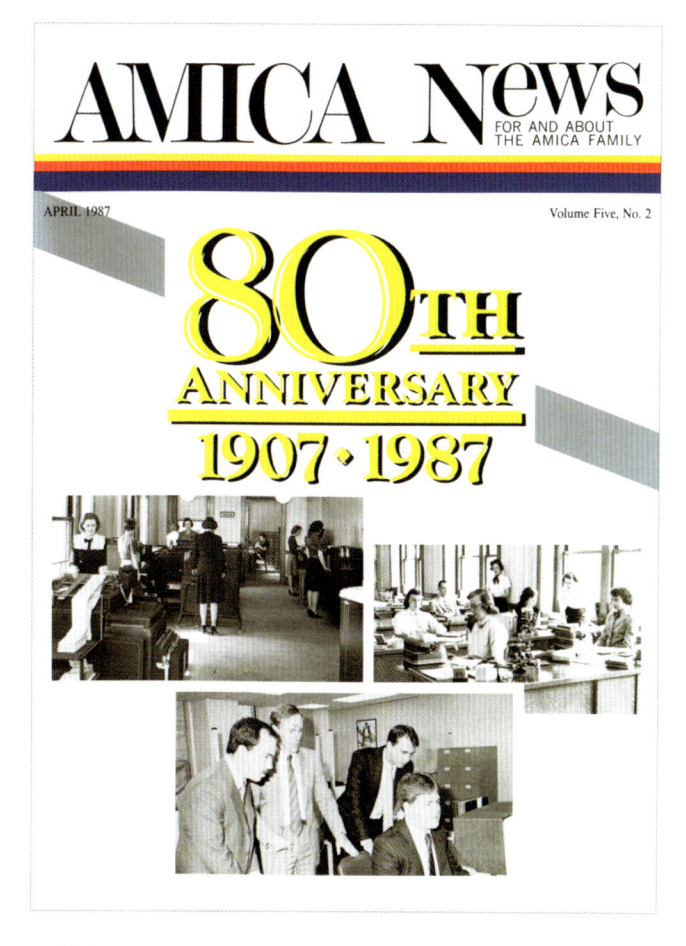

In 1987, Amica celebrated 80 years of loyal service to its policyholders.

them there, staged, ready to go when the time comes. We set our expectations high.[21]

In May 1985, fires devastated the retirement community of Palm Coast, Florida, and within weeks tornadoes tore through portions of Ohio, Pennsylvania, and New York. While losses to Amica policyholders in both cases were "mostly minor," these incidents provided Amica employees with a chance to prepare for greater catastrophes in the months and years to come.

"In both cases, branch employees contacted insureds in the area before policyholders called in themselves," the company reported. "Lists of insureds were organized immediately, and letters and phone calls went out one or two days after the catastrophes occurred."[22]

In September 1985, Hurricane Gloria made landfall at Fire Island, New York, 40 miles northeast of Manhattan, and blew through Connecticut and Massachusetts. Amica insured 120,000 homes there, as well as many cars and boats. Fortunately, Gloria's winds, which at one time reached a destructive 150 mph, dropped below 100 mph by the time it made landfall. Amica policyholders filed 6,477 claims, which would have totaled approximately $6.2 million in losses in today's economy. As Bob Hanke explained, "We really lucked out. Even though this was the largest storm we had ever faced, ... it could have been so much worse."[23]

In order to respond to policyholders in the wake of Hurricane Gloria, Amica utilized a catastrophe (CAT) team—a strategy that the company would employ frequently in the coming years.

CAT teams include adjusters, supervisors, and clerical support personnel with previous catastrophe experience, and the teams essentially operate as a separate branch office.[24] For two to three weeks, crews tirelessly work to bring things under control. Any claims not settled by the team in the field can be handled by the local office afterwards.

In 1989, CAT teams played important roles in Amica's response to Hurricane Hugo in the Carolinas and the massive earthquake that hit Northern California in October. In the case of Hurricane Hugo, weather predictions actually allowed Amica to have a CAT team in place before the Category 4 hurricane even came ashore.

Hurricane Hugo caused massive damage to the Carolinas, snapping trees and utility poles like twigs, damaging boats, and destroying thousands

The owner of this boat filed one of the 6,477 claims resulting from Hurricane Gloria, which ripped through the Northeast Atlantic states in September 1985.

Amica paid tribute to its employees in 1988, the year its assets exceeded $1 billion for the first time. That year, the company was also singled out in a book titled *The Service Edge*, which recognized 101 American companies that excelled in service.

of homes. Amica policyholders filed approximately 355 auto claims, 900 homeowners claims, and 50 marine loss claims. By the end of 1989, losses to Amica from Hurricane Hugo totaled more than $3.6 million.[25]

In October, just a few weeks after Hugo ravaged the eastern seaboard, a catastrophic earthquake measuring 7.1 on the Richter scale struck the West Coast. Fires raged, highways buckled, buildings collapsed, and homes toppled in Central and Northern California.

The company responded to the situation immediately and, within an hour, arrangements had been made to send a team to the area. Computer scans were developed to determine the areas of greatest risk, policyholders' coverage plans were reviewed, and additional office space was set up to accommodate the extra personnel necessary during the emergency. Just 12 hours later, the company's San Rafael Office was open and operating.[26]

With phone lines down in much of the area, Amica received few incoming policyholder reports, and employees decided to initiate contact with policyholders in the affected areas. Less than four days after the deadly earthquake, Amica made contact with all policyholders with earthquake coverage in San Francisco and Santa Cruz counties. The resulting 121 home claims and 40 auto claims revealed that Amica's policyholders were spared from the worst of the earthquake's damage. The company's paid losses at year-end totaled about $675,000.[27]

Overall, while Amica policyholders fared better than expected after Hurricane Hugo and the California quake, those two catastrophes contributed to making 1989 the costliest year in history for the insurance industry, with losses nearly 2.5 times higher than the previous record.[28]

Tobey wrote in the annual report that the events of 1989 gave Amica an "opportunity to shine—to rise to the occasion and prove that our reputation for service is well-founded. ... In spite of the catastrophes, which drained nearly $8 million in claims payments and reserves, our net profit for the year was solidly within the parameters of our expectations."[29]

Just two years later, however, "nature hit Amica harder in 1991 than in any other of its 85 years. Fire, ice, wind, and water battered policyholders as never before."[30]

That year, an ice storm hit the Rochester, New York, area in March, and Hurricane Bob whipped southeastern New England in August, costing Amica $7.2 million for 5,177 claims. Yet the worst catastrophe of the year came in October, when wildfires destroyed large areas around Oakland, California.[31] The devastation was described as:

October 20, 1991—a quiet Sunday becomes a roaring inferno for thousands of people living in the hills overlooking Oakland, California, and picturesque San Francisco Bay. The wide-ranging blaze is so intense that homes actually explode, and cars are melted into driveways. Returning homeowners describe the smoking remains as "chimney graveyards" and "World War II London."

An Amica CAT team member (left) helps a policyholder's son search through debris for anything that might still be intact after a 1991 wildfire in Oakland, California.

The conflagration took the lives of 25 people and left behind eerie residential wastelands.

Amica records only 41 auto and homeowners insurance claims, but with homes valued at prices ranging to $500,000, claims losses exceed $4.2 million. ... Total insurance industry losses due to the devastating blaze are approximately $1.5 billion, qualifying this ... as one of the costliest fires of the past century.[32]

On the whole, Amica's 1991 catastrophic losses, before adjustment for reinsurance, set a new record of more than $19.5 million and provided the company another opportunity to demonstrate that an Amica insurance policy is security policyholders can count on.[33] In spite of natural disasters, a weak economy, and modest premium growth, Amica still turned a profit.[34]

Hurricane Andrew

In the spring of 1992, an Amica CAT team spent almost three weeks in Dallas, Texas, after a hailstorm pummeled the Dallas–Fort Worth area. The April 28 storm proved the costliest in Texas history, with total insured losses estimated at $460 million, according to news reports. The resulting 960 claims cost Amica $3.5 million.[35] Later that year, Hurricane Andrew, one of the worst storms in American history, slammed into South Florida.

At approximately 3:00 A.M. on Monday, August 24, Hurricane Andrew's heavy winds began pummeling the area for the next six hours. The storm's effects were devastating. About 250,000 people were left homeless, and hundreds of thousands had no electricity or running water.

Amica responded immediately. Jim Teevin arrived at the Coral Springs Branch Office by 8:30 that morning. Since the phones were operational, Teevin called employees to see who could make it to work. By the end of the day, the office had already logged between 400 and 500 claims. Within a day after the storm, Amica sent 16 people, the largest CAT team ever assembled, to assist with the recovery, doubling the size of the Coral Springs claims staff. Working in tight quarters, the team began the first of several weeks working 12 hours a day, seven days a week.[36]

Don Murray, who was with the Glastonbury, Connecticut, branch office and was the coordinator of the first CAT team, arrived with several other team members on August 25. "It wasn't until we settled that we realized how bad the devastation really was," Murray said. He also recalled how emotionally draining it was for the people taking phone reports:

Some broke down because the stories were so upsetting. ... We were issuing advance money for additional living expenses—checks for up to $10,000—over the phone. That's the most we could do in the beginning. We just wanted to get the policy-

Andrew Through the Eyes of a CAT Team

AS THE ACCOMPANYING PHOTOS DEMONstrate, both taken by members of the Amica CAT team in the aftermath of Hurricane Andrew, team members not only provide a vital service to policyholders, they also experience firsthand the physical, psychological, and financial effects of major catastrophes. This understanding is, and always has been, at the root of Amica's commitment to customer service.

From the first days of the Automobile Mutual Insurance Company of America, the company has prided itself on going above and beyond the call of duty to take care of its policyholders. During the 1980s and early 1990s, as a series of hurricanes, hailstorms, brush fires, and earthquakes affected Amica policyholders around the country, Amica's commitment to service reached a new level with the formation of catastrophic response teams, known as CAT teams. Groups of Amica employees are flown into afflicted areas to ensure efficient claims coverage as the regular Amica employees in the area work overtime to keep up with the vast amounts of work generated by a disaster.

While Amica had always maintained lists of experienced property adjusters who would be sent to afflicted areas in the aftermath of catastrophes, in the 1980s, CAT teams were officially created and readied for action.

The importance of these CAT teams was evident in 1992, when Hurricane Andrew, "the most devastating United States catastrophe of the century," hit South Florida and Louisiana.[1] Within a day of the storm, the first members of Amica's largest CAT team to date arrived.[2] The 16 team members spent endless hours in the ensuing weeks helping policyholders restore order to their lives.[3]

The devastating aftermath of Hurricane Andrew offered Amica employees and CAT team members another chance to work diligently on behalf of policyholders, a tradition the company has maintained since its inception in 1907. With the help of formalized CAT teams, Amica can continue to provide excellent service to policyholders in the midst of disaster.

holders settled somewhere if they couldn't live in their homes. We dealt with the hurricane's devastation around the clock, even in our hotel. It was filled with homeless families and their pets.[37]

Hurricane Andrew proved to be the most devastating catastrophe of the century for the United States.[38] The insurance industry faced record-breaking total losses in excess of $16.5 billion. According to the American Insurance Services Group, 1992 became the worst year yet for property and casualty insurers in terms of catastrophes.[39] Amica also saw its highest catastrophe losses ever, with more than $41 million in losses for Hurricane Andrew alone. Other disasters during the year brought Amica's total for catastrophe losses in 1992 to $58 million, of which $25 million was recovered from reinsurers.[40]

Amica's efforts to quickly honor the substantial claims resulting from Hurricane Andrew renewed policyholders' loyalty to the company. As Bill DeForge, who had been with Amica since 1965, explained:

I think we showed our true colors during Hurricane Andrew in Florida, which was just an awful event. Other insurance companies came out of that with some horrible publicity. Amica came out with glowing reviews. Some of the letters that peo-

Below and inset: Photos taken by the Hurricane Andrew CAT team showcase the damage in the area, where 250,000 people were left homeless and hundreds of thousands were without electricity. Hurricane Andrew was the United States' most devastating catastrophe of the 20th century, with total losses exceeding $16.5 billion.

Hurricane Andrew allowed Amica to demonstrate its commitment to customer service with its largest CAT team ever. The team worked 12 hours a day, seven days a week, for several weeks.

ple sent in ... were almost heartbreaking in terms of the devastation, but they spoke of how we were able to step in and put the pieces back together. I feel very good about that, and I'm sure that as long as there is an Amica, that will always be the case.[41]

In his "Message to Our Policyholders" in the 1992 annual report, Tobey took pride in the fact that Amica had once again not only survived, but thrived, during a difficult year:

Amica celebrated its 85th anniversary during 1992, and if ever there was a testimonial to the virtues of the Amica business style, that year was it. ... Repeated tornadoes, Hurricane Andrew, and the most powerful Northeast coastal storm of the century all took their toll and profoundly reminded us of the nature of our business. Despite the many major catastrophes, we finished the year with our reputation strengthened and all of our vital signs strongly intact.

There was more good news during our 85th anniversary year. Once again, Amica was named No. 1 in the nation in an evaluation of auto insurers conducted by one of the nation's foremost consumer publications. And Amica was the first property/casualty insurance company in the country to receive the new highest rating (A++) awarded by A.M. Best company.[42]

Looking to the Future

Even as Amica dealt with the numerous catastrophes of the late 1980s and early 1990s, the company remained focused on its own progress and growth. During the summer of 1989, work began on a new office park, and the first two buildings in the complex, No. 10 and No. 25, were completed and occupied by the fall of 1990.[43]

The 87-acre suburban office park, located outside downtown Providence, was part of a company cost-containment effort and soon became the new home for more than half of the Home Office staff. The new location featured lower per-square-foot expenses for office space, free parking for all employees, drive-in claims service, and convenient access to major highways. The *Amica News* described the rationale behind the move:

Of particular benefit is our ability to achieve greater efficiency of operations by the most opportune positioning of interrelated functions.

We recognize that we must be creative and willing to take bold, new steps to maintain our service reputation and the affordability of our products. Our new Operations Center has been designed and opened in furtherance of those two historic Amica performance prerequisites.[44]

The suburban office park was situated on a beautifully landscaped tract of land in Lincoln, Rhode Island. With construction of the new five-story, 125,000-square-foot West Campus Building, due for completion in the spring of 1993, Amica sold its 40 Westminster Street building in December 1991.

The sale enabled Amica to move several more departments out to the Lincoln Center Office Park and assured Amica "the capacity to accommodate long-range growth right through the turn of the century," said Joel Tobey.[45]

By the end of 1992, as the new West Campus Building neared completion, the company reported on the progress and noted a significant decision made by Amica's board of directors:

Previously known as the West Campus Building, the building now has a new name and address— 35 Lincoln Center Boulevard. ... "Although future plans focus on an Amica campus, with all Home Office employees located at the Lincoln site, the company has no current proposal to erect another building," according to Mr. Tobey. "However, the concept of selling the 10 Weybosset Street building has been approved by the company's board of directors, and if a buyer were found, plans would proceed with the construction of another building."[46]

By the end of June 1993, 420 employees had moved from the 40 Westminster Street building to

Left: The company celebrated the new A++ rating from A.M. Best in August 1992.

Right: Amica marked its 85th year in business in 1992, the same year Hurricane Andrew devastated South Florida.

the new building in the Lincoln Center complex.[47] In December of that year, Amica sold the Home Office building at 10 Weybosset Street in Providence, the same building that had once housed the "one small room" in which the Automobile Mutual Insurance Company of America was founded in 1907. The company planned to "leave 10 Weybosset Street behind" and relocate its headquarters to the new Lincoln Center Office Park within three years.[48]

In December 1993, Amica reported on the substantial changes it was undergoing, while highlighting its long-standing commitment to quality:

This has been a year of challenge, an exciting chapter in the history of our company. The move to the 35 Lincoln Center office building was suc-

cessfully completed, along with the sale of the 10 Weybosset Street building.

We can proudly reflect upon a year filled with achievements made possible by your efforts. Of particular significance was the No. 1 rating our Homeowners Insurance received in Consumer Reports' *national survey of its readers. The magazine drew replies from more than 240,000 readers.*

"*Amica received the fewest complaints,*" *the magazine stated.*

Mr. Tobey wrote in a memo to employees, "I cannot stress enough the importance of this recognition. The consistency with which we receive Consumer Reports' *top rating clearly demonstrates that our commitment to service is an inseparable part of our corporate culture. It is this single characteristic that continually separates us from our competition. However, to be successful in the future, we must perpetuate our reputation for exceptional customer service."*[49]

The move to Lincoln continued in phases. In October 1994, Amica occupied a one-story building in an industrial office park next to the Lincoln campus. The building, located at 20 Blackstone Valley Place, would serve as temporary office space for three years while planning and construction continued on Amica's newest building, 45 Lincoln Center Boulevard. Also that month, Amica announced that "all remaining departments in the 10 Weybosset Street building (except the Rhode Island legal department) would relocate to Lincoln Center Office Park by year-end."[50] The *Amica News* described the transition:

In the waning days of December, most remaining Amica employees located at the 10 Weybosset Street building were emptying desks and packing boxes in preparation for their relocation to the Lincoln Center Office Park. There was a hint of sadness as they left Amica's birthplace behind. The move marked the end of almost 90 years of operations in downtown Providence.

The 45 Lincoln Center Boulevard building, a seven-story, 170,000-square-foot corporate headquarters, will house corporate executive functions, claims and underwriting executive departments, and the investment and accounting departments. The facility, which will also include a spacious dining area and a 100-seat amphitheater, will be completed and occupied in mid-1996.[51]

In April 1995, the Rhode Island Federation of Garden Clubs, Incorporated, awarded Amica a citation for the environmentally sensitive development and landscaping of the Lincoln Center Office Park, noting that:

The complex was designed with a sensitivity toward natural features and living things seldom found among large-scale development projects in Rhode Island. ... While buildings, travel lanes, and parking lots occupy more than one million square feet, their impact on the Lincoln landscape is subtly

The *Amica News* celebrated the first phase of the company's move in 1990 to the beautifully landscaped site in the suburbs. By the end of the next year, Amica had also sold its building at 40 Westminster Street and relocated several more departments.

muted by extensive plantings of trees, turf, and shrubs. ... Preservation and protection of native woodlands and wetlands are found throughout the property. ... The result is the creation of an 87-acre office park with enormous aesthetic and recreational appeal for both employees and visitors.[52]

At the groundbreaking ceremony in July 1995, the Lincoln Center Office Park became the largest office park in Rhode Island, home to more than 1,300 Amica employees. Rhode Island Governor Lincoln Almond spoke at the groundbreaking ceremony. "Amica is a tremendous asset to Rhode Island," he said. "It's a success story for the whole state."[53]

The March of Technology

Since Amica purchased its first computer in the early 1960s, the company's reliance on tabulators decreased drastically through the years. At one time, tabulators were used for processing dividend checks, billing, accounts receivable, and other extensive tasks. In September 1984, Amica marked the "end of an era" as tabulators became obsolete and were discarded in favor of computers.[54]

As technology continued changing rapidly, Amica's data processing department took on more and more responsibility. By 1986, the data processing department was in need of a new title to "more accurately describe the function of the department in today's business environment." The *Amica News* noted:

Almost 25 years have passed since Amica entered the field of data processing. Mr. Abel Sr. established a systems and programming section within the tabulating department in November 1961, with a staff of five people. The first computer, an IBM 1410, arrived in February 1963 and was

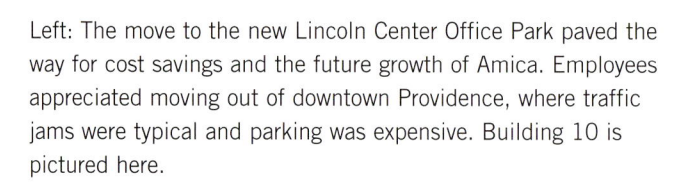

Left: The move to the new Lincoln Center Office Park paved the way for cost savings and the future growth of Amica. Employees appreciated moving out of downtown Providence, where traffic jams were typical and parking was expensive. Building 10 is pictured here.

Below: Amica employees tour the 87-acre suburban office park, which soon became the new home for more than half of the Home Office staff.

FAREWELL TO 10 WEYBOSSET STREET

DURING THE MID- TO LATE-1980s, TWO factors led Amica executives to consider moving the company from its downtown Providence location. It became exceedingly clear that, as Amica continued to grow, more office space would be needed. In addition, traffic jams in Providence increased commute time, and employees faced expensive downtown parking costs. Relocating to a spacious, low-traffic suburban area with free parking seemed an optimal solution. The company set its sights on a beautiful tract of land in Lincoln, Rhode Island.

The new location was a drastic change from the famous "one small room" at 10 Weybosset where A. T. Vigneron established Amica in 1907. In that same building, eventually purchased and renamed the Amica Building, the company's staff grew from two clerks to almost 3,000 employees.

Amica executives, including A. T. Vigneron, DeForest Abel Sr., and Joel Tobey, had paced the hallways and ridden the elevators of that historic building. During the Hurricane of 1938, Amica employees had watched refrigerators bob down the river from those windows, and after the Blizzard of 1978, they had taken in "refugees,"

Employees began moving into the Lincoln Center Office Park in the fall of 1990.

people unable to make it home after the storm, feeding and housing them for days.

The decision to sell the original Home Office was not taken lightly. However, according to Tobey, Amica needed room to grow to remain "technically and professionally postured to meet the needs of our growing family of policyholders."[1] In December 1993, Amica sold 10 Weybosset Street. By the end of December 1994, Amica had moved all Home Office employees to its new headquarters.

With the new 87-acre suburban office park finally complete, Amica had met its goals of creating a campus that allowed for growth, streamlined efficiency, and a superior work environment for Amica employees. The new office park included a company fitness center, parks, and walkways. In addition, it created an atmosphere that remained faithful to the integrity and tradition of the original Home Office. Amica may have left 10 Weybosset Street, but the "one small room" ideals and traditions would never leave Amica.

In 1993, company President Joel Tobey (second from right) and Bill Schwab (far right) from human resources joined fitness center representatives at the opening of Amica's corporate fitness center for employees.

put to work rating and renewing New York automobile policies in July 1963. By August 1967, the name of the department was changed to data processing and several underwriting departments ... had been introduced to the computer age.

The most recent change occurred in January 1986, when the department changed its name to corporate information systems.[55]

The new corporate information systems department consisted of 230 employees on four floors at 10 Weybosset Street and played "an integral part in [Amica's] working day."[56]

In 1987, Amica began using computers to help with two more important tasks. The company reported that employee time cards were to be replaced by an automated system: "Amica has simplified its record-keeping procedures by switching from time cards to an automated computer system. The time cards, although accurate, involved mailing, sorting, and storing 135,000 cards annually. Additionally, it was necessary for the personnel and payroll departments to keep duplicate attendance records for each employee."[57]

Later that year, Amica took another important technological step with the debut of computerized word processing:

Ever since the first Amica insurance policy was tapped into the memory of a computer, the question of how to get the most out of those bits of information has been rolling around in the minds of our underwriting staff. ... [Now we have] developed a computer letter-writing program [that] is putting information from policy records to work.

Before computer letter-writing, underwriting employees who took policyholder calls had to dictate confirming letters. Much of the information already in the computer had to be repeated to the word-processing operators so they could address the letter properly. ... Today many policy changes can be processed by our customer service representatives while they are still on the phone with policyholders. The stroke of a few keys on their desktop terminals is all it takes.[58]

Maintaining the Culture

Despite the many changes, Tobey kept employees firmly focused on the special company culture that had kept Amica successful for so long.

According to Bryan Cook, who was hired in 1989, "The company just has a pervasive customer service nature, and everything is focused around service to the customer. [When I joined Amica, I] didn't meet anybody who had been there for six months. Everybody had been there for 10, 20 years."[59]

Ken Nails joined the company in 1990 and recalled Amica's sense of business ethics:

I knew that Amica was good. ... I didn't believe how good. I had worked for a couple of insurance companies before going to the Alliance, and then I came here. Once, a policyholder complained about something, and ... [Mr. Tobey] said, "Find out what happened, and get back to him and answer the question."

I thought, "You are responding every time an individual policyholder writes in or asks a question. This is not a normal insurance company."[60]

Bob DiMuccio, who worked previously for an accounting firm that had Amica as one of its clients, joined the company in 1991 and later became president and CEO. While working outside the company, he recalled having a positive impression of Amica's culture and standards:

> When I started as a company employee in 1991, Harold Hitchen said to me, "Even in the accounting department, you drop everything for a policyholder." I think it was on my first day. The accounting department normally does not have direct policyholder contact. Our contact would be infrequent, usually involving a billing issue, and he said, "You drop everything for a policyholder."[61]

The satisfaction that employees felt in working for a company that treated both employees and policyholders with great respect was reflected in the fact that by April 1995, Amica had 18 employees with more than 40 years of seniority with the company.[62] These long-term employees played a critical role in passing down Amica's traditional values to new hires.

Two Notable Retirements

The early 1990s saw the retirements of two employees who contributed greatly to Amica's success: Clayton Koelb in 1991 and Earl Chambers in 1993.

Clayton Koelb was a senior executive vice president when he retired after almost 42 years with Amica. He had the deepest respect for Amica and its employees and a lifelong dedication to the company's financial well-being. He said, "I am extremely proud to have worked for a company whose ethical standards are above reproach. The company has always been eminently fair in its dealing with employees, policyholders, and claimants."

Earl Chambers was a senior vice president in the investment department when he retired in 1993. "Amica's investments were in good shape when I came in, and I'm leaving them in the same shape," he said. "I have always said that when you pass through a place, if you can't make it better, just don't make it any worse." This was quite an understatement considering that Amica's investments flourished during the 20 years Chambers was overseeing the company's securities.

Joel Tobey took over the presidency of Amica at a critical time and steered the company soundly through a period of incredible change and growth. By 1994, he was ready to step down, and Thomas A. Taylor, who had been with the company since 1970, was elected president and CEO.[63]

In December 1994, Tobey explained the move to employees in "A Holiday Message from the President":

> My upcoming retirement offers a perfect example [of how careful planning] can ... ensure a smooth transition into the future. Planning for that change

Rhode Island Governor Lincoln Almond (left) joined Amica executives including President Thomas Taylor (right) at a groundbreaking ceremony for a new building at the Lincoln Center Office Park in 1995.

began many months ago. Now, not only do we have strong new leadership in place, but the implementation of our strategic plan will allow us to meet the future head-on.

As I reflect upon my career at Amica, I feel fortunate to have worked for such a fine company and, more importantly, with such a wonderful group of people. Please allow me to take this final opportunity to thank you for your support and dedication to Amica. Without you, we surely would be just another insurance company. I wish each of you continued success at Amica.[64]

Dr. Lowell Smith, a member of the board of directors from 1982 to 2004, recalled that: "When Joel Tobey was elected, he knew the company as well as anyone could know it, and he had a vision of this company in a far different setting from 10 Weybosset Street. He had a vision of a campus and a far more productive environment."[65]

Peter Goldbecker, who would later become a senior vice president and corporate secretary, recalled how Tobey implemented his strategic plan for Amica:

He felt it would be an excellent idea for Amica to become focused as a company, rather than [having] individual divisions and departments work on strategic goals. Tom Taylor, who was his assistant, and then eventually Andy [Erickson] were brought over to work on this project, and they spent [a massive amount of] time and effort developing the first set of goals for the senior officers and for the company.

Mike Labbadia and Bob Livingstone pose next to a tabulator. Amica retired the last of its tabulators—the machines that were used to process dividend checks and for billing, accounts receivables, and other tasks—in the mid-1980s.

CHAPTER SEVEN: JUST THE BEST

Representing a changing of the guard, outgoing President and CEO Joel Tobey, on the left, shakes hands with incoming President Thomas Taylor in this photo from the 1994 annual report.

That was really a landmark, and then as time went by, we refined the process. We also broke down the barriers of having an underwriting executive only be concerned about underwriting, and claims only being concerned about claims, and then we began to have some cross-divisional goals that involved a number of departments or divisions. ... It led eventually into the growth that we're sustaining right now and when Tom Taylor took over as president.

[Tobey] was very interesting and exciting to work for. He thought things through. He knew how to get things done, and he had the drive and energy to begin to change the direction of the company.[66]

The *Amica News* bid farewell to Tobey in the December 1994 issue: "Although he is retiring, Mr. Tobey will continue as a member of the Board of Directors. As CEO, Mr. Tobey promoted a strong sense of pride, integrity, and teamwork throughout the company and always gave credit to the Amica family for its part in the company's growth and progress. Through his leadership, Amica has been guided to its enviable place in the insurance industry."[67]

Amica's new president, Thomas Taylor, had his own vision of how to maintain Amica's "enviable place in the insurance industry" and to keep the company growing while maintaining the core Amica values Tobey worked hard to uphold. Taylor would pursue his vision during a decade of even greater change.

On November 17, 2006, J.D. Power's Jeremy Bowler (center), senior director, and Scott Quarderer (right), director of insurance services, presented Robert A. DiMuccio with Amica's two newest J.D. Power awards. Amica has received a total of 13 J.D. Power awards as of 2006.

CHAPTER EIGHT

INTO THE MODERN ERA
1996–2007

After you have spent 90 years building the best insurance company in the industry, what do you do next? If you're Amica, the answer is this: You take the best and make it even better.

—Thomas Taylor,
President and CEO

DURING THE MID-1990s, AS A new century loomed on the horizon, a new president took charge of Amica, and the company continued the process of moving into a beautiful new office park in suburban Lincoln, Rhode Island. Thomas A. Taylor, elected president at the annual board meeting in 1994, worked to maintain the company's focus on its long-held traditions of steady growth and firm commitment to customer service.

After graduating from Bryant College, Taylor began his career working as a claims adjuster at another insurance company. "When I first joined Amica on April 1, 1970, April Fools' Day, I sat in the office filling out forms and tuning in to the conversations that were taking place around me. I actually paused and thought, 'These people really do take customer service seriously.' It was palpable, the atmosphere with regard to service. Things were just not let go. Phone calls were promptly returned. Appointments were kept. We have a saying here: 'We are a company that keeps its promises.' It was true then, and it is true today."[1]

Twenty-four years later, Taylor, clearly steeped in Amica traditions, was elected president, a move employees greeted with great enthusiasm. As the 1994 annual report put it, "How appropriate it is ... that Joel N. Tobey, the retiring president, rose through the ranks via the underwriting side of our business, while Thomas A. Taylor, the incoming president, comes to us from claims. Since both career paths converge on the essentials of insurance and customer service, the transition from one leader to the other can do nothing less than assure us of the continuity of professional progress."[2]

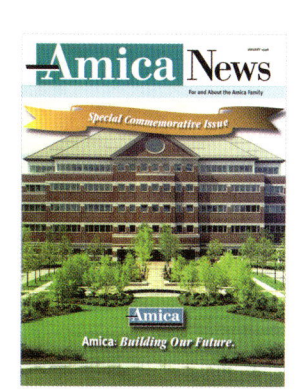

When Taylor became president, it was apparent to everyone at Amica that he had not forgotten the lessons he learned during his first days with the company. Ken Amylon, who joined Amica shortly after Taylor in 1972, remembered how important the Amica tradition of customer service remained to the incoming president. "For years, Mr. Taylor carried the *Consumer Reports* article from 1962, which was the first time that we were favorably mentioned in *Consumer Reports*," Amylon said. "Now he is able to tell people we have never been pushed out of first place in the Consumers' Union survey in over 40 years."[3]

Taylor understood that preparing Amica for the 21st century without compromising the company's founding ideals required the determination of the entire Amica staff. From his very first days as pres-

---

The completion of Amica's beautiful office park in Lincoln, Rhode Island, as shown in this special commemorative cover of the *Amica News* from January 1998, was greeted with praise.

ident, he remained intent on maintaining a friendly, constructive work environment for employees.

Taylor instituted a system in which he and other top-level executives traveled to every branch office at least once every three years. With 42 branches open around the country, this created a rigorous travel schedule. As Amylon described it:

> I think it is really a credit to Mr. Taylor that he has stuck to this schedule and persevered, even when people have asked him, "Would once every five years be enough?" He decided that it was a priority for him. I will tell you, when you are in the branches, it is really energizing. It is very worthwhile.[4]

Although Taylor, a marketing major in college, clearly understood the importance of Amica tradition, he also had a revolutionary idea for moving Amica into the 21st century. He believed that Amica should begin advertising, a strategy that proved to be one of the boldest in the company's history.

The Advertising Age

Since the company's founding in 1907, Amica grew and thrived based solely on word of mouth. Rather than buying advertisements in newspapers, or on radio and television, Amica relied on its policyholders to pass along their recommendations to people who would make desirable policyholders. This concept of "preferred risk" was enormously successful for the company. However, as Taylor explained, Amica needed to become "far more aggressive with regard to seeking out new business. There was a time when you could not become a policyholder unless you were recommended and checked out. I'm very happy to say that back in the mid-1990s, around 1996 or so, we became far more aggressive in regard to seeking out new business."[5]

The idea to begin advertising was originally introduced in 1992, while Taylor worked as superintendent of claims, as part of conversations about the need for Amica to engage in serious, long-term planning. He recalled:

> [In 1993], knowing that Joel Tobey was going to be moving into retirement in a year or so, I said I wanted to bring over a fellow named Andy Erickson so that he and I could work together on our strategic corporate plan. We held a major strategic planning retreat with about 27 senior officers and generated a strategic plan that had essentially

CHAPTER EIGHT: INTO THE MODERN ERA

During its first 90 years, Amica placed no advertisements. Instead, the company relied on individual policyholders' word of mouth to spread news of Amica's top quality work to others. In 1998, however, Amica launched a national advertising campaign to bolster recognition of its name and help stimulate growth.

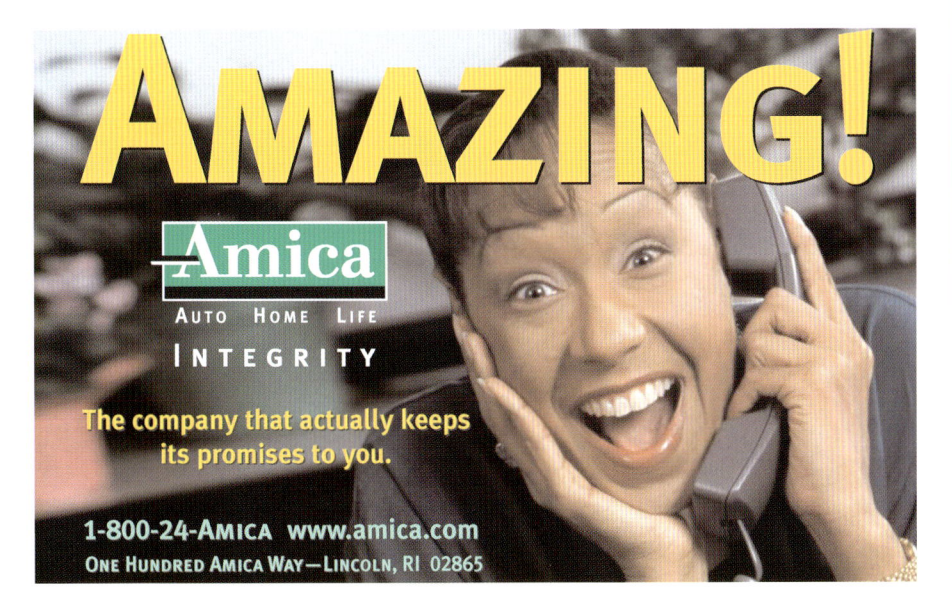

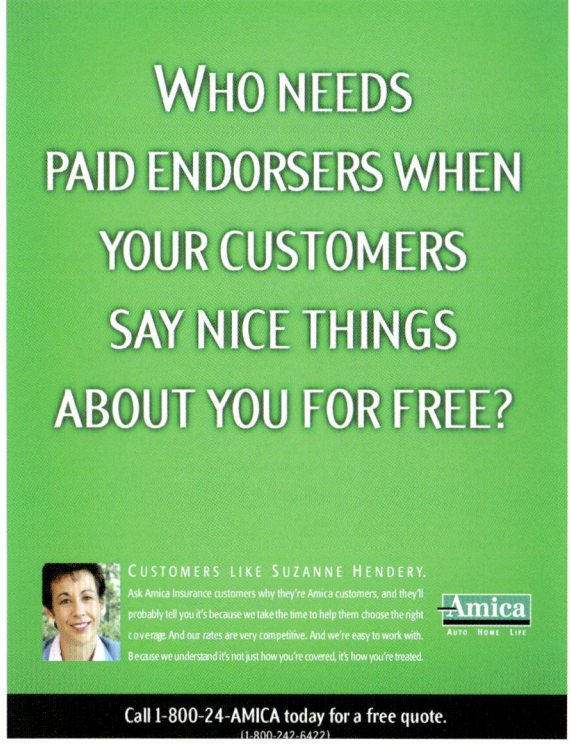

only five key initiatives to it, but about 150 operational objectives. We kept building on that plan year after year.[6]

Taylor and the other Amica executives decided by late 1995 that Amica should concentrate resources on marketing, advertising, and sales. The best way to do that, they decided, was to bring in an outside consultant. Amica hired a division of KPMG to study the distribution of Amica products and develop a strategic marketing plan. It would prove, in Taylor's words, "the best thing we ever did. A turning point in this company, as far as I'm concerned."

Soon, Amica decided to focus on television advertising. Taylor continued:

We went to our board and said, "This is what we would like to do: We want to start advertising on television." Well, we had never done anything like that. It was foreign to us. We had no advertising. Our first year out, we had an advertising budget of about $27 million, and we developed a focus. We said, "Okay, we are a great East Coast company, and we are pretty well known in the Northeast. However, because of catastrophic risk exposure, we really need to grow our policyholder base in parts of the country that are less catastrophe-prone." ... We decided to focus on the Midwest, the Northwest, and the Southwest, and we hired a local advertising agency, Rivers, Doyle & Walsh, as our first advertising agency.

In 1997, Amica announced the new marketing strategy to its employees. "Amica has implemented plans to achieve growth," Taylor wrote. "Specifically, in 1998, we will launch our first-ever advertising campaign to bolster recognition of the Amica name and help stimulate growth. A series of television ads will be supported by radio and magazine ads, along with direct mail campaigns."[7] Taylor explained:

Where do we grow in 1998 and beyond? How are we going to get there? In 1997, Amica conducted a comprehensive review to address these questions, and the results of our research indicated that, although our company is well-represented in many states, a need exists to communicate the Amica story in a meaningful and memorable way to potential new customers in areas where Amica is less well known.

Thomas A. Taylor

WHEN THOMAS A. TAYLOR WAS ELECTed president and CEO of Amica in early 1994, he had a clear vision of what Amica needed to do: move rapidly into the modern era while preserving the founding principles that made the company successful. This proved to be a challenging task, but one Taylor, who understood both the Amica way of life and the challenges of doing business in modern America, was eminently suited for.

Taylor graduated from Bryant College in 1963 and started his career as an adjuster at another insurance company. "The work really appealed to me because of the nature of investigative work," he recalled. "Also, the freedom of the road was a terrific allure to me, and the most difficult day of my life was when I was promoted to a claims supervisor and had to come in off the road and turn in my company car!"

Before starting at Amica, Taylor worked across the street from the Amica Building, in Providence, Rhode Island. He quickly became aware of Amica's reputation for fairness and integrity, both in his professional dealings with Amica and in the friendships he developed over the years with Amica employees.

"The thing that struck me about Amica, apart from the very rigid dress code that existed back in the 1960s, was the high degree of professionalism at Amica," he explained. "The dialogue I would have with Amica's claims adjusters, at that time, indicated that they had much more reasonable caseloads and that they took their service responsibility very seriously."

Taylor joined Amica in 1970 as a claims adjuster and rose quickly through the ranks. He worked in the Rhode Island claims department for several years, becoming manager in 1975, assistant vice president in 1977, and senior assistant vice president in 1986. He was transferred to the claims executive department and promoted to senior vice president and superintendent of claims in 1988, and in 1992, he transferred to the corporate executive department and was appointed executive vice president.

Upon his election as president and CEO in 1993, Taylor implemented a new strategic planning process for Amica.

"We came to a recognition in late 1995 and early 1996, through our strategic planning process, that we really needed to get out of the Dark Ages when it came to marketing, advertising, and sales," he said.

In the coming years, Taylor guided Amica through many changes. Amica would develop initiatives in advertising and marketing that would drive the company to ever-greater success.[1]

The new Amica Home Office was featured in the 1997 annual report, with the headline: "Amica: The Rebirth of a Notion."

[One important part] of our plan calls for the creation of image-building advertisements for print, television, and radio. Historically, Amica has grown through word of mouth and referrals. Beginning this year, we will augment our growth with marketing strategies that include the use of television and radio advertising in areas where we do not yet have an established presence. Although both the media and the methods we use may be new for Amica, the overall goal remains the same as always: to help the company grow by adding careful, responsible individuals to our family of policyholders.[8]

According to Taylor, advertising was just the beginning. Amica soon began finding new ways to improve its public stature. He continued:

We have modernized our graphic identity. We have expanded the facilities at our corporate office park in Lincoln, Rhode Island, and renamed the office park Amica Center and its streets Amica Center Boulevard and Amica Way. We have found more appropriate names for our national network of offices, selecting names for greater location recognition. With a Strategic Marketing/Advertising Plan, we have embarked upon an exciting new effort to unify and strengthen our identity across America. ... This is only the beginning.[9]

Advertising proved a drastic change for some Amica employees. Mark Divoll, who joined the company in 1977, recalled the changes he had witnessed: "I don't think Amica even listed itself in the Yellow Pages because it didn't advertise. And now we would not only be listed in the Yellow Pages but also have TV, radio, and print ads. It was a total change."[10]

Frank Maaz, who joined Amica in 1972, recalled that the decision to begin advertising "raised some eyebrows, especially among some of the old-timers. Maybe I was one of them."

However, he soon changed his mind. "You have to see the handwriting on the wall at some point and say, 'Referrals have worked really well for us for the last 90 years or so, but maybe we need to do a little more because the rest of the world is changing around us,'" he explained. "We are not immune to that."[11]

Three television commercials debuted in February 1998. One advertisement focused on automobile insurance, another on homeowners insurance, and the third on name brand recognition. The ads were initially broadcast in five markets where Amica saw potential for expansion of its business: Milwaukee, Wisconsin; Albany, New York; Knoxville, Tennessee; Rochester, New York; and Portland, Oregon. Throughout 1998, the commercial broadcasts expanded to 11 other areas.[12]

Bryan Cook of the personal lines products division recalled the first time he saw an Amica commercial outside an NBA playoff game in Indianapolis in the late spring of 1998. "The game was sold out, so the Pacers put big-screen TVs on the streets outside so that people could get down there and watch the game," he said. "At halftime of the game, the Amica commercial played on the big screen outside Market Square Arena, and we received some good feedback on that. ... It was amazing."[13]

The new marketing campaign proved successful. According to Stuart Towsey, executive vice president, who joined Amica in 1973, the marketing campaign was "absolutely fabulous." He continued:

It's a great thing to see that someone has at least heard your name. Before the ads, we were the No. 1 company in the United States for service, and yet no one ever heard of us. Unless you ran into an insured somewhere, you just didn't hear about us. I think it has been fabulous that they have taken that step to make the Amica name known. ... The campaign was very successful, increasing our growth actually almost to the point that it was too much. ... As an organization that prides itself on making certain that we have trained, educated people answering the phone, we wanted to make sure we had those people available before all of these new policyholders started calling. It is a very good problem to have.[14]

Even as Amica grew rapidly with the influx of new policyholders brought on by the advertising campaign, the objective and motivation of the company remained. In the words of Steve Brainard, Amica Life senior assistant vice president, Amica remained "constantly oriented toward what is right for the customer, and toward doing a great job rather than being the largest company around."[15]

According to Steve Holland of the corporate services department, the Amica focus on customer service comes "from the top, and it is constantly driven home." He recalled his father, Joe, who also worked for Amica, explaining to him that "Amica has very high standards. The policyholder is No. 1. [We] bend over backwards for the policyholder and never compromise our standards." For Holland, one of the most important aspects of Amica is its "culture of empathy, of putting ourselves in the shoes of the policyholder."[16]

Ron Rainer, retired, put it succinctly. "Without a question in my mind, Amica has the best people anywhere," he said. "You look forward to coming to work in the morning. People who work for Amica embrace this whole culture—service to the company, service to others, service to our clients."[17]

The culture of empathy became an integral part of the Amica advertising campaign. As Bruce Maynard explained, "I can dress you up in different clothes tomorrow, but you are going to be the same person at the core." In other words, the advertising campaign did not change Amica's values. It served only to make many more people aware of those values.[18]

A New Home, A New Look

As Amica moved forward with its marketing strategy, the company also completed work on its office park in Lincoln, Rhode Island. By August 1997, the "majestic" flagship building, which "drivers can see rising just over the treeline from the

1923 **1935** **1939** **1957** **1998**

highway," was almost 80 percent complete. When finished, the building totaled nearly 172,000 square feet and featured a campus courtyard consisting of a "formal fountain area with bench seating, numerous trees and plants, and two formal gardens that will serve as pleasant gathering places for Amica employees."[19] The building was ready for occupancy by the end of 1997.

In February 1998, Amica renamed the Lincoln Center Office Park the Amica Center, and at the same time, introduced its new logo to the world. In February of that year, President Thomas Taylor wrote:

It is my distinct pleasure to officially introduce our new company logo. It represents our many strengths in a bold, contemporary fashion. Its introduction coincides with the renaming of our office park to Amica Center, and its streets to Amica Way and Amica Center Boulevard. ...

I would like to take this opportunity to offer my special thanks to all of you for your hard work, your energy, and your commitment to what we know is America's very best insurance company. Whether you are among the more than 1,100 Rhode Island employees I have the pleasure to greet on a regular basis or the nearly 2,000 employees who staff the 39 Amica offices beyond Rhode Island's borders, I extend my wholehearted appreciation for your personal contribution to Amica's ongoing success.[20]

In May 1998, Amica conducted a dedication ceremony for the new flagship building, now known as the 100 Building. The *Amica News* stated: "Seen from the highway or from the gentle green of Amica Center, Amica's new 100 Building is simply majestic. Its 260,000 bricks were laid in place after countless hours of planning and construction. This building, Amica's new Corporate Headquarters and the focal point of the beautiful Amica Center campus, is so much more than just office space. It

Throughout its history, Amica's name has always been synonymous with quality and professionalism. Its appearance, however, has undergone several changes. In 1998, Amica unveiled a dynamic new logo that reflects the company's financial stability. The new logo was also designed to maximize the company's brand identity and connect all company communication efforts.

represents the hopes and dreams of generations of employees."[21]

Beyond its physical beauty, the new building had "great significance to all of us here at Amica" and was "much more than simply bricks and mortar," Taylor explained at the ceremony. "We hold this event with no small degree of pride. Our dedication to a pleasant office environment is so strong, it is one of the five guiding principles included in our Statement of Mission."[22]

Integrity and Community

In the late 1990s, as the stock market swelled, Amica enjoyed the prosperity sweeping the country and grew at an unprecedented rate. As countless insurance and financial companies merged and became publicly traded entities, Amica stayed true to its roots. In 1998, the board of directors reaffirmed its commitment to remain a mutual company—one owned by its policyholders. As Taylor explained in the 1998 annual report:

Demutualization of insurance companies and megamergers between large insurance and financial companies are a fact of life. They make headline news, and no doubt we will be seeing more of them. However, your company, Amica, is unequivocally committed to its mutual organization.

Amica does not have any stockholders or outside investors of any type. As a mutual company, we exist to serve your needs and work exclusively for your benefit. ... We have developed a comprehen-

The Success Sharing plan, originated in 1997, quickly became an important part of the Amica culture, highlighting the company's commitment to its employees.

sive long-term business strategy that involves prudent growth, adhering to core competencies, focusing on personal lines products, and keeping personalized service in high gear. Unlike the megamergers, these plans are not the stuff of headline-making news. However, they exemplify the kind of levelheaded approach to business that has caused so many policyholders to stay with us for a lifetime. This philosophy has precipitated a string of high industry ratings. A.M. Best, the leading insurance industry analyst, has awarded us the highest possible rating for financial stability repeatedly. Amica has been included in the Ward's 50 Benchmark Group. ... Most recently, Amica was awarded an AA+ rating from Standard & Poor's for our superior financial performance.[23]

Bob Benson, senior vice president and Amica's chief investment officer, explained, "From my first day here, the whole emphasis of the Amica investment strategy was that the policyholders own the company, and that is who we report to. That is what we focus on. That is our concern. As I sit in the senior staff meetings and the board meetings, that is still what they focus on. Everything, every decision, is based on what is good for the policyholders. Decisions are never based on, 'Well, how is this going to maximize profits?' That kind of thinking does not enter the equation."[24]

This thoughtful investment strategy ensured that when the stock market bubble burst in the late 1990s, Amica would weather the fallout. It also indicated Taylor's awareness of the values that guided Amica to its great success, values he reinforced at every opportunity. The 1999 annual report featured a message from Taylor, titled "An Amica Policy: Making Ethics a Priority." Considering the numerous corporate scandals that garnered negative media attention at the start of the new millennium, such dedication to morality proved important in maintaining a positive company image. Taylor wrote:

> Ethics are of utmost importance in the business world. The decisions and actions of employees ultimately determine the reputation of the business for which they work. Even entire industries can be affected by the choices made by just one company.
>
> Amica has always appreciated that its policyholders have a deep trust that we will make our decisions with ethics in mind. We never take that trust lightly, and we have made our commitment to ethics a company priority.[25]

Amica management understood the importance of rewarding employees for their continuing commitment to customer service and wanted them to share in the general success of the company. With that in mind, Amica executives created a new program called "Success Sharing" in February 1997. Through this program, Amica employees directly share in the financial success of the company by receiving cash bonuses when Amica has a successful year.[26]

CHAPTER EIGHT: INTO THE MODERN ERA

This year-end bonus program, which grew out of suggestions offered by Amica employees, proved very successful in 1997. Eligible employees received a bonus equaling 6 percent of their 1997 regular earnings. Although generally favorable weather conditions and a lack of major catastrophic events helped Amica achieve financial success in 1997, the efforts of a vast array of employees also contributed to the banner year.[27]

Success Sharing quickly became a fixture at Amica, adding, as Taylor would write in 2002, "a palpable spirit of teamwork, dedication, and commitment that permeates our company at every level" and from which "flows the company's success. … I can think of no better way of demonstrating our commitment to the Amica family of employees than by sharing with them the financial success they helped create."[28]

Amica did more than look after the financial well-being of its employees. In 1995 and 1996, thanks to the company's emphasis on employee safety, fitness, and wellness programs, Amica received the highest honor among the Worksite Health Awards, sponsored by the Greater Providence Chamber of Commerce, Blue Cross & Blue Shield of Rhode Island, and the Worksite Wellness Council of Rhode Island.[29]

In the late 1980s, the company also introduced an Employee Assistance Program (EAP) to help employees deal with the hectic pace of life in the late 20th and early 21st centuries. The free and confidential service serves as a referral agency with a countrywide network of professionals and resources to assist Amica employees and their families.[30]

Amica once again turned its attention to improving customer service. As Taylor wrote in the 1999 annual report:

Service will continue to be a high priority area at Amica. Although we continue to receive accolades for service excellence on a national scale, we are not relaxing. We will continue to implement new methods of providing exceptional service. Two methods

Below: Amica's Web site, www.amica.com, provides information, billing services, and insurance quotes for new and existing customers.

Right: The staff of the new National Customer Service Center in 1999 included, clockwise from top left, Jaclyn Jerome, Erin Weir, Roxanna Adams, Lori Desrosiers, Linda Ahlert, and Joyce Prior.

employed last year include the significantly improved www.amica.com Web site and our National Customer Service Center. Both of these steps will help us to service our insureds whenever and however they need us.[31]

The National Customer Service Center was launched out of conversations about customer service that took place in 1998. The center opened on the Amica campus in Lincoln, Rhode Island, in 1999. Lee Valentini recalled the center's beginnings:

Up to that point, our backup after hours was local answering services, and then we would have adjusters who would be on call. If your house was on fire, God forbid, you would call, reach the answering service, and they would page an

Some of the corporate information systems employees responsible for successfully implementing Amica's Y2K plans have their photo taken for the 1998 annual report.

J.D. POWER RECOGNIZES QUALITY

IN THE EARLY YEARS OF THE NEW CENtury, Amica continued to rack up numerous awards for customer satisfaction and the overall quality of its insurance products. Some of the most prestigious honors were bestowed in 2006, when the company received J.D. Power and Associates' ranking for Highest Customer Satisfaction Among National Auto Insurers for the seventh year in a row, and for Highest Customer Satisfaction Among National Homeowner Insurers for the fifth year in a row.

Established in 1968 by J.D. Power III, J.D. Power and Associates is a global marketing information firm and business unit of the McGraw–Hill Companies that conducts independent and unbiased surveys of customer satisfaction, product quality, and buyer behavior. Power started his marketing firm to define marketing problems, conceptualize solutions, and provide management with the information to achieve results. The firm soon became nationally recognized as a credible source of information, and in the early 1980s, J.D. Power and Associates generated its first Customer Satisfaction Index, which demonstrated that quality remained the key requirement for customer satisfaction.

Today the firm's services include industry-wide syndicated studies, proprietary tracking studies, media studies, forecasting, training services, business operations analysis, and consulting on customer satisfaction trends.

With its team of more than 750 professional analysts, statisticians, economists, consultants, experts in demographics and consumer behavior, and administrative support personnel, J.D. Power and Associates is best known for its work in the automotive industry. In recent years, however, the firm has expanded to serve a number of other industries including telecommunications, travel and hotels, marine, utilities, healthcare, home building, consumer electronics, and financial services.

Today, J.D. Power and Associates is the gold standard in measuring customer satisfaction, and Amica—with its string of "Highest" ratings—has proven that, even while facing the intense challenges of the 21st century marketplace, it maintains the highest standards of customer service in the insurance industry.

---

adjuster. You would still be in contact with Amica, but it was going through these channels. However, the way the market was moving, people expected to be able to contact us and that we would write policies after hours and on weekends. ... Silvana Klara, who came from the underwriting/production side, [worked with me] to start it up. I was appointed manager and she, assistant manager. We took six or eight experienced employees, and when we started, we worked from five to midnight, Monday through Friday. On Saturdays we worked 8:30 to 4:15 just to try and catch up on those telephone calls.[32]

In 1999, Amica introduced Access Amica at the Amica Web site, which served as a "digital extension of Amica's national branch office network," providing both an additional level of service for existing policyholders and a new point of access to the company for potential policyholders.[33] In 2000, the Amica Web site expanded to include online billing and online quotes for homeowners insurance.[34]

Amica further enhanced its communications with customers by launching a quarterly newsletter in 1999, titled *Amica Today*. The publication provided beneficial information to policyholders and

Left: Diversity ambassadors were assigned to every branch and corporate office department as part of Amica's strategic efforts. The *Amica News* highlighted their accomplishments.

Below: Pat Wesolowski of the corporate information systems department was among employees volunteering at a special fundraising telethon in Rhode Island.

informed customers about various types of coverages offered by Amica.

The company's commitment to customer service and corporate integrity inspired an ever-increasing array of accolades. In January 1999, Amica earned the top spot in a *Consumer Reports* ranking of insurance companies offering homeowners coverage, and in September of that year, it shared first place in a *Consumer Reports* survey of customers' satisfaction with their automobile insurance.[35]

"What is truly remarkable is that for the 28 years that *Consumer Reports* magazine has been ranking insurance companies, we have never had less than their top rating," Taylor noted in a communication to employees.[36]

The following year, Amica ranked highest in customer satisfaction in the auto insurance industry in a J.D. Power and Associates study, the first of seven uninterrupted years in which Amica would earn that prestigious honor.[37] In the fall of 2001,

Amica was included for the sixth consecutive year in the Ward's 50 Benchmark group, which analyzes more than 3,000 property and casualty insurance companies to recognize excellence in balancing financial safety, consistency, and performance.[38]

While the company modernized its marketing strategies and rededicated itself to customer service, Amica and its employees remained active in community service. In 1996, the company created the Amica Citizenship Grant Program, awarding 33 grants to people and organizations intent on making a difference in communities across the country.[39]

In 1997, Amica announced the creation of the Amica Companies Foundation: "In addition to expending a tremendous amount of energy and resources to achieve corporate growth, Amica has always had a strong social conscience. In 1997, the Amica Companies Foundation was established to provide funding to worthy charitable organizations. The Amica Companies Foundation will go a long

Throughout the 1990s, Amica and its employees continued to participate in community service. Here, employees help build a house as part of a Habitat for Humanity project.

way toward achieving our corporate philanthropy objectives for many years to come."[40]

Throughout the late 1990s and early 2000s, Amica and its employees worked with nonprofit organizations and participated in community projects, including the Pawtucket (Rhode Island) Family YMCA, a "Rock and Roll Marathon" to benefit the Leukemia Society in San Diego, a United Way raffle, the Greater Danbury (Connecticut) Lions Club, the American Cancer Society, the North Shore Cancer Walk in Massachusetts, the Children's Miracle Network Telethon, and the March of Dimes WalkAmerica.[41]

In 1999, Amica employees contributed their time and money to at least 21 charitable organizations across the country, underscoring Amica's commitment to not only its policyholders, but the communities in which they live.[42]

In 2003, Amica created a program for high school students titled, "Navigate Your Fate," which enabled students to learn about the impact of alcohol on their reflexes and judgment. Participants wore special goggles to simulate the effect of being drunk while attempting a series of activities, such as driving a golf cart through a secure course of orange cones, throwing a basketball, and walking a straight line. Communications Officer Patti Stadnick praised the program for raising awareness among teenagers on the consequences of intoxication, pointing out that "students can discover how it feels to try and perform these tasks while they are impaired, without actually being impaired."

In November 1998, Amica conducted its first Diversity Works Conference, which was designed, in part, "to reaffirm Amica's commitment to recognizing, respecting, and appreciating the differences existing within the Amica family," and "to heighten awareness of the company's movement toward a workforce and policyholder base more representative of a cross section of American society." Employees from every branch office were trained to help support and create awareness of diversity issues among their coworkers. According to Taylor, "An increasingly diverse workforce is necessary if we are to understand and meet the needs of our increasingly diverse customer base."

Specialty-trained employees were dubbed "diversity ambassadors." To this day, every branch office and corporate office department has one or more employees who are responsible for bringing diversity awareness to their coworkers.

To celebrate their diversity, employees have enjoyed a variety of programs, including "diversity luncheons" featuring foods representing the varied cultures of all those present. Some employees have also been treated to presentations by coworkers wanting to share interesting aspects of their personal heritage.

In an increasingly diversified nation, a multicultural workforce and customer base are critical. "It was eye-opening to realize how diversity issues could affect future business practices," said one ambassador during a diversity luncheon held in early 2000 by the Amica Life company featuring foods from China, Greece, Portugal, and Italy.[43] Amica's efforts to create an increasingly diverse workforce continued into the new century and are still in effect today.

Taylor took the reins of Amica in the mid-1990s with a clear goal in mind: to bring Amica into the modern era without compromising the company's bedrock ideals of community and integrity, while continuing to grow at a prosperous and reasonable pace. By the early years of the new century, Amica had attained that goal while continuing to plan for a bright future.

The Day the World Changed

The terrorist attacks of September 11, 2001, profoundly altered the way many Americans viewed the world. Not only were they forced to look beyond their borders to understand the forces affecting their lives, but, simultaneously, the boom economy of the late 1990s officially ended. Americans found themselves in a time of political and economic uncertainty. Despite—and perhaps because of—these new challenges, Americans came together in the aftermath of the devastating attacks.

In the wake of the tragedies, Amica faced many of the same challenges as individuals and businesses across the country. As in so many times of crisis throughout its 95-year existence, Amica rose to the challenge of helping those most in need. The Amica family went straight to work. "With thoughts

---

In the wake of the terrorist attacks of September 11, 2001, Amica joined in the national effort to support the victims of terrorism.

of victims, volunteers, and very dedicated rescuers fresh in mind, the Amica Family has turned anguish into action," according to a December 2001 report. The report continued:

> *Amica quickly turned its attention to the needs of two important groups of people—Amica customers and the families directly affected by the tragedies in New York, Pennsylvania, and Washington, D.C. The first job was to check in with customers who might have been affected.*
>
> *Amica's Danbury Regional Office, right on the doorstep of New York City, started working right away, making as many phone calls as possible, despite overloaded lines and downed cell phone towers, to customers in affected areas.*
>
> *The office's actions generated an unsolicited response from policyholder Dylan Seff: "One of the first calls I received after escaping the tragedy of the World Trade Center attacks ... at home in Manhattan was from my local Amica branch office. To ease some of what was an incredibly horrible and stressful time by offering help and financial assistance was an enormously positive surprise, as I did not even realize I was covered for this sort of thing."*[44]

Amica's response went beyond its own policyholders. Given Amica's culture of service, employees also reached out as individuals to assist victims' families and relief organizations. In response, the Amica Companies Foundation took an unprecedented step, forging a resolution to match employee donations to the American Red Cross' New York City/Washington, D.C., relief efforts. After offering active employees and directors the opportunity to donate for a three-week period, employees and the foundation contributed a total of $170,500.[45]

In a memo to employees, Taylor said, "I am overwhelmed by the generosity of Amica's employees and directors. You are all heroes in my eyes. ... If we support each other and stand together as one people, the events of September 11 will help us grow stronger."[46] In his President's Message in the 2001 annual report titled, "Meeting Change with Integrity," Taylor wrote:

Frederick Kast, in the Rhode Island claims department (left) was among employees helping load a truck with supplies for suffering New Yorkers.

> *The year 2001 was one of the most tumultuous in recent memory. The terrorist attacks of September 11 profoundly affected us all as we watched the tragedy unfold in New York City; Washington, D.C.; and southwestern Pennsylvania. Fortunately, Amica did not incur significant financial losses stemming from the tragedy, but the colossal loss of life and property inspired us to contribute to relief efforts.*
>
> *Apart from the events of September 11, the property and casualty insurance industry sustained its worst losses due to natural disasters in the second quarter. Tropical Storm Allison hit Texas especially hard, and June hailstorms wreaked havoc in the Midwest. Factor in last year's lackluster economy and most would expect*

a fairly bleak outlook, but thankfully there is much good news to report.

In a difficult year for our industry, our economy, and our country, Amica's conservative financial strategy, commitment to policyholders, and core values provided strength and stability. We have once again proven that Amica can "weather the storm."[47]

The Modern Era

Amica moved forward in the post-9/11 world by focusing on the same values that had guided it through its first 95 years of prosperity. Even as the company dealt with the attacks and the troubled economy, it expanded the National Customer Service Center to include a call center in Spokane, Washington, to provide "continuous 24-hour availability to handle customers' needs."[48]

The next few years proved difficult for the American economy, especially since a record-breaking hurricane season in 2005 devastated large regions in the South. However, Amica continued to prosper, and the company's customer service and sustained growth continued to earn accolades.

In 2003, J.D. Power and Associates ranked Amica "Highest in Customer Satisfaction Among

Helen MacNeil, senior vice president in the personal lines products division, said keeping up with changing state insurance regulations is challenging.

National Auto Insurers" for the fourth consecutive year and "Highest in Customer Satisfaction Among National Homeowner Insurers" for the second year in a row. "This is an accomplishment that no other insurance company can claim," according to the Amica annual report for 2003. "It is truly an outstanding achievement and speaks volumes about our employees' commitment to go above and beyond in servicing our policyholders." Also in 2003, the A.M. Best Company once again rated Amica Mutual Insurance Company A++ Superior, its highest rating, and paid tribute to Amica for earning its top rating for 50 consecutive years.

Amica continued the tradition of garnering top ratings, and in 2004, 2005, and 2006, J.D. Power and Associates awarded the company its fifth, sixth, and seventh awards for "Highest Customer Satisfaction Among National Auto Insurers." J.D. Power and Associates also awarded Amica its third, fourth, and fifth consecutive awards for "Highest Customer Satisfaction Among National Homeowner Insurers" during 2004, 2005, and 2006.

The new era also brought rapid change and technological advances. The swift evolution of the insurance industry presented unique hurdles. Helen MacNeil, senior vice president in the personal lines products division, said that one of the most important aspects of her job is keeping up with constantly changing state insurance regulations.

According to Steve Dolan, vice president of Amica Life, the pace of change is also a challenge. "Nowadays, the marketplace changes much more rapidly than it did 20 years ago," he said. "Whereas before we put out a new product once every three, four, or five years, now some companies put them out every six months."

Another critical aspect of doing business in the 21st century involves the speed of technological advancements. Amica augmented its mainframe computer systems with PC-based client-server systems in the late 1990s, and the pace of change continues to quicken. "It is a global community or village," explained Dave Kenny, an Amica employee for more than 20 years. "With communications as they are, the pace of technological change in terms of computer systems is very rapid."[49]

The Amica Life Company works to be at the forefront of technological change. As Dennis Giordano, retired, explained, "We are putting systems online so that customers can apply for life insurance, pay bills, and complete applications right on the Internet. You can see your policy values online, [in] real time, up to the second on our Web site."[50]

With technological advances come even more challenges. In 2003, Amica introduced Identity Fraud Expense Coverage—a new coverage for a new era. As *Amica Today* explained, "To help tackle [the problem of identity theft], Amica introduced the Identity Fraud Expense Coverage endorsement for new and renewal homeowner, condominium, and renter policies. It provides first-party coverage for expenses incurred by an insured as a direct result of any identity fraud first discovered or learned of during the policy period."[51]

Even with all of the new technologies and types of coverage, Amica remains focused on the same core values. As Peter Cameron of the personal lines products division explained:

> *The pace of things that happen has just absolutely gone through the roof. ... Society has sped up dramatically. It is a symptom of the times we live in. However, people are what is important, people are the center of things, and people have not changed that much. We have had to add some new products that help them with various aspects of their lives, but the nuts and bolts of what we do really has not changed.*[52]

Amica's marketing efforts continued in the 21st century, and included Amica's sponsorship of the National Geographic IMAX film, *Forces of Nature*. The film focused on the formation and impact of severe weather, such as tornadoes, earthquakes, and volcanoes. Amica ran a 60-second advertisement at the start of the film, educating audiences about the role of an insurance company in helping policyholders recover from damage incurred by a natural disaster.

"We felt that a film on the forces of nature was a good match for us," explained Margaret Munroe, retired. "We sponsored that film and premiered it in about 20 theaters across the country, creating a disaster preparedness kit to be handed out at the premieres and inviting first responders, including police, fire, and emergency management professionals."[53]

Amica continued to prosper as the company changed. By 2003, the company's assets reached $3.13 billion, and in 2004, Amica had 42 offices around the country and 3,300 employees.[54]

Thomas A. Taylor successfully met his goals. Amica's social conscience remained stronger than

Amica's spirit of community service, from the cover of the October 2002 edition of the *Amica News*.

Helping Hurricane Victims

THE 2005 HURRICANE SEASON PROVED to be the most active in recorded history, and one of the deadliest as well. Powerful storms whipped across the Atlantic, leaving thousands dead, destroying cities, ruining crops, and devastating portions of Louisiana, Florida, Alabama, and Mississippi, as well as areas in Cuba, Haiti, Mexico, and the Bahamas. Damage costs reached a record-breaking $100 billion, and more than 2,000 lives were lost.

On August 25, Hurricane Katrina struck South Florida with 80-mile-per-hour winds, spawning destructive tornadoes, flooding cities, and killing 14 people. The fast-moving storm reached the Gulf of Mexico six hours later, strengthening to a Category 5 within days. Then, on August 29, the storm slammed into Louisiana and Mississippi with winds reaching up to 130 miles per hour and a 30-foot storm surge that caused devastating flooding as far as Mobile, Alabama. An estimated 80 percent of the city of New Orleans remained underwater for days afterwards, and more than a thousand people died in Louisiana alone. According to The American Insurance Services Group (AISG), insured losses totaled $38.1 billion, with total losses exceeding $75 billion, twice the amount sustained during Hurricane Andrew in 1992.[1]

Amica suffered only moderate losses as a result of Hurricane Katrina, and the company donated $100,000 to the American Red Cross to help provide basic necessities such as food, water, and shelter. "The human needs go beyond Amica policyholders and are enormous," explained President and CEO Bob DiMuccio. "As part of Amica's efforts, we will also match individual donations up to $1,000 made to the American Red Cross by any Amica employee." All together, Amica donated $325,000, including $112,000 in individual employee contributions. CAT teams were sent to the affected areas to assist with claims, and Amica used before and after satellite images of neighborhoods to help assess damage levels and provide service to policyholders.

"Claims volume increased steadily every day," said Brian Cremer. "We soon discovered that insureds had fled to many states, some quite distant. Our initial response was highly focused on the need to help with the additional living expenses that these families incurred. We began to issue claim cards immediately, and were sending them via UPS for prompt delivery. We ultimately issued more than 200 claim cards to help with additional living expenses in a span of just two weeks. Many of us worked the entire Labor Day weekend to assist as many insureds as possible." According to

Left and opposite: The 2005 hurricane season wreaked havoc in Florida and along the Gulf Coast, costing $100 billion in damages and killing more than 2,000 people.

Ted Murphy, vice president of claims, Amica was the first property and casualty insurance company to make available "instant-issue" claim cards to their insureds.

Since many of the parishes in Louisiana had no electricity or telephone service for weeks following the storm, CAT teams made personal unannounced visits to policyholders. "The response we received was tremendous," Cremer said. "Policyholders were amazed that we had visited them even if claims had not been reported. The adjusters commented that they had never before experienced the hospitality and warm welcome they received from our insureds."

Regional offices in Houston, Atlanta, and Tampa handled most of the claims and incoming calls. Shameen Awan, who worked in the Atlanta Office at the time, recalled Katrina victims calling in tears as they described their losses. "You really feel for the people living in that area," she said.

As time passed, the true scope of the devastation became clear. Cremer described the difficulties hurricane victims faced:

> Most people we talked to were unable to return home to inspect the damage. The severe flooding and lack of power, water, and sewage treatment facilities rendered southern Louisiana a war zone. Families had to confront the reality of being displaced for months. They had to enroll children in schools while they lived in temporary accommodations and with extended family in different cities and states. The emotional stress of trying to keep a household together under these circumstances became very evident to us as we discussed these issues with insureds. No one had been prepared to be away for more than a few days. The human story here was just beginning to unfold.

Unfortunately, in September, the region suffered another direct strike from Hurricane Rita, further complicating efforts. The storm surge caused major flooding in Louisiana, Texas, and Mississippi, completely destroying several coastal communities and escalating flood conditions in New Orleans.

Only a month later, on October 24, Hurricane Wilma struck the west coast of Florida with 120-mile-per-hour winds, ruining valuable crops, damaging homes, and toppling trees. According to the National Hurricane Center, total insured losses approached $6.1 billion.[2] Although insured loss totals were far below Hurricane Katrina's losses, Amica faced much greater costs as a result of Hurricane Wilma.

"We experienced the largest CAT event in Amica's history with Hurricane Wilma," explained Paul Pyne. "Wilma produced $56 million in claims that have been paid and reserved compared with $42 million in claims paid and reserved for Hurricane Andrew, the second most significant CAT event. Wilma resulted in 5,300 claims, … more than twice the number of claims that were reported after Hurricane Andrew."

According to Pyne, the dedication shown by claims specialists and employees made a real difference as hurricane victims attempted to rebuild their lives. "Our sincere thanks and gratitude to all of those employees who participated in handling these CAT claims," he said. "It is because of their work that Amica has again delivered on the promise of providing excellent service to our insureds during their time of need."

ever, the company had grown and prospered, employees were well-schooled in diversity issues, and the company's advertising program thrived. With Amica enjoying the fruits of those accomplishments and others, Taylor announced his impending retirement late in 2004.

A Sacred Trust

In February 2005, after the retirement of Thomas A. Taylor, the Amica board of directors elected Robert A. DiMuccio president and CEO. He graduated from Providence College in 1979 with a Bachelor of Science degree in accounting, and joined Amica in 1991 as a vice president in the accounting department, earning a promotion to senior vice president in 1994 and treasurer in 1996. In 2001, he became chief financial officer, and in 2003, he was named executive vice president.[55]

According to DiMuccio, Amica's service, ethics, and loyalty set Amica apart, and he believes they remain the keys to the company's future success. One of his main goals is to maintain Amica's traditional values far into the future. He explained:

I feel a sacred trust. [Amica] is a special place. ... The company is approaching its 100th year, and I want to make sure that we move the company forward and get ready for its next 100 years. I truly hope there is somebody sitting in this seat 100 years from now. The company will look very different, I would suspect. It will adopt the technology and methods of the time period, but I hope the ethics are still here. Now that is what I see as my goal—to propel Amica into its next century of existence.

Amica's solid reputation helped the company remain successful, DiMuccio added. "It is my job to move the company forward and become larger and more prosperous, building its reputation for service to a higher level than it is now, and then passing it along to the next generation of management in the same way that it was passed to our generation," he said.[56]

DiMuccio's priorities for ensuring Amica's growth include shifting the company's marketing strategy. With insurance industry growth, in the words of DiMuccio, "really flat in the last couple of years," Amica shifted its marketing focus in the early months of 2005 from image and brand marketing to direct-response advertising.[57] Once potential customers call, DiMuccio pointed out, Amica's customer service and competitive pricing will make them Amica policyholders.[58] DiMuccio maintained:

We continue to update our policies to make them state-of-the-art for our customers, adding coverage

Above: As technology advances, Amica works to keep up with new challenges. This issue of *Amica Today*, from the summer of 2003, highlights the problem of identity theft.

Right: Maribeth Williamson, senior vice president and treasurer, said that Amica has always been committed to maintaining the highest ethical standards when it comes to financial matters.

Amica sponsored the National Geographic IMAX film *Forces of Nature* as part of its new advertising campaign.

where we think it's necessary and where coverage enhancement makes the policy more desirable. We plan to provide just plain better coverage for individual risks—everything from identity theft coverage to our homeowners platinum coverage, which covers many homeowner risks that are either covered in much smaller amounts or not covered at all by a standard homeowners policy.[59]

With the insurance industry going through "a major change in the way products are priced," DiMuccio made it a priority that Amica implement a new pricing system for both auto insurance and homeowners insurance.[60] In 2005, Amica began the process of rolling out a new pricing system.[61]

"You have to enhance pricing sophistication to survive in this marketplace," explained Helen MacNeil. "If you want to attract the best risks, you have to have the best prices for those people, or they will go somewhere else."[62]

The new rates, however, required a whole new rating system for Amica. The new homeowners insurance rating plan, for example, incorporates factors such as the number of people living in the home, the number of claims they have had in the past, their credit history, and how long they have been insured with Amica.

"We essentially went from one rating cell to 544 rating cells just based on a matrix of years insured, number of claims, and credit," said MacNeil. "It has been unbelievable the amount of cooperation we have had with the corporate information systems department."[63]

In Amica Life, Jim McDermott, senior vice president and general manager, noted that in 2004, "We sold over $6.2 million in life insurance premiums, which was a record year by far. The most we had written before was just under $5 million." He attributed the record-breaking performance to new initiatives in sales technology and needs-based sales training, along with the shift in advertising focus.[64]

Keeping up with the rapid advances in technology remains a priority for Amica. DiMuccio advocates Amica's increased use of the Internet as a tool for interacting with customers. He also extended call center hours so that 24-hour assistance is available.[65]

A new telephone system employed by Amica in 2005, known as ASPECT, is designed, in the words of Paul Pyne, senior vice president and superintendent of claims, to "turn all of our branches into a virtual call center." He continued:

When telephone activity has reached a high volume, a call will be forwarded to an employee who is available to respond more rapidly to that call. The call will be sent to a branch. If that branch has high telephone activity and there are no employees available, that call will bounce back to another location so it can receive a prompt response. Instead of being dependent on a branch-by-branch staffing situation, we better utilize our employees countrywide. Our hope is to do a better job with our telephone expense management while enhancing service by more promptly responding to telephone calls.[66]

Pyne explained another way in which new technologies maintain competitiveness:

We are working on establishing electronic claims files, a paperless claims file for the future.

After the retirement of Thomas Taylor, Robert A. DiMuccio, a Providence, Rhode Island, native, became Amica's latest president and CEO in February 2005.

This requires managing many different elements, from imaging documents so that they are digitized, to deciding how we want to present that information to our employees. The ultimate goal is to have an automated assignment feature so that when a policyholder calls in, we will take a first notice of loss and then that claim will automatically be assigned to the Amica employee best able to help that policyholder.[67]

This electronic system enjoys the added bonus of providing Amica employees with electronic notes, so that as they contact policyholders, they can simply add notes to the electronic file instead of having to complete additional paperwork.

"We recognize and feel that we have the best employees in the property and casualty business," Pyne added. "Now we are trying to give them the technology that they need to make sure that we maintain cutting-edge service."[68]

As Executive Vice President Stuart Towsey explained:

In the last year, we have come to the forefront by focusing on the competitiveness of our organization relative to the insurance industry. For years, we set ourselves apart from everybody else and actually did not feel many of the competitive issues that face many other insurance companies. We had our own little niche, our own little culture, and we were somewhat insulated from some of these other processes.

Competitive pressures in all realms of the corporation are so much greater today, and we are now impacted by them. ... We are trying to hold on to the things we value as a culture in our company and, at the same time, meet the expectations of the insureds of today, which are so much different from what they were just a few years ago.[69]

What Makes Amica Different

In 1984, a young job seeker named Vince Burks answered an ad for a sales position and soon found himself in an auditorium full of people. "There were a couple hundred people in there," Burks said. "There was a stage, music, and balloons. It was quite a production. I ended up sitting toward the front. This person comes out on the stage and tells us about all the money we are going to be making, ... but never tells us what the product is. Then he pulled out a vacuum cleaner and said, 'You are going to be selling vacuum cleaners door to door.' I was not happy. I immediately left."

Burks next went to Executive Search, a professional placement firm, where a gentleman talked to him for a while and then asked, "Have you ever thought about working in the insurance business?"

Burks had not, and the man told him about Amica. Burks did some research and heard from several people that Amica was the cream of the crop when it came to customer service and its excellent treatment of employees. He landed an interview, and despite the fact that he had stumbled across Amica "by accident," he has been with the company for more than 20 years.[70]

Burks' experience is one he shares with many Amica employees. Attracted by the Amica culture, many remain for the length of their careers.

CHAPTER EIGHT: INTO THE MODERN ERA

According to Pat Talin, senior vice president of human resources, the average Amica employee tenure is 10 years.[71]

What is it about the Amica culture that brings people in and keeps them there, and how has Amica maintained this culture throughout a century of growth and change?

Mark Divoll, who joined Amica in 1977, explained: "I'm sure you have heard of the Amica Family taking care of the employees, from the work environment to the benefit packages. I think that even with all the changes in business, these things at Amica are still superior to those of other insurance companies."[72]

There are other equally important factors that aid Amica in retaining employees. "An important part of maintaining our culture is the way we treat each other," Talin said. "We go to lunch with our management trainees after their six-week training program and ask them what made them decide to come to Amica. Many of them say, 'When I came to the Home Office for my interview and people walked around with me, they said hello to everyone by name.' It is an outgoing, friendly environment."[73]

According to Russ Furlong, who joined the company in 1972, from their very first day at Amica, new employees are "trained in a certain way to do it right, take your time, and treat the customer how you would like to be treated. ... In the morning, when I'm shaving, I'll look at myself in the mirror and think that I'm a decent person, and I'm trying to do a good job. That is what I do. Treat customers the way I want to be treated."[74]

Tom Buckley, an Amica employee since 1977, agreed. "When you get hired here, one of the things that they tell you is that we are never going to ask you to do anything that is not ethical," he said. "If you make a mistake, we are not going to take your head off."[75]

Jim Ruegg, who joined Amica in 1984, added:

Below left: Stuart Towsey, executive vice president, believes that the future looks very good for Amica.

Below right: Paul Pyne, senior vice president and superintendent of claims, said technology, including a sophisticated new phone system, is helping Amica keep its edge over the competition.

If it is gray, we do not do it. We do not look for ways to try to fudge and try to get around something. In the 20 years I have been with Amica Life, I can count on both hands the number of complaints that have been filed against us.[76]

Maribeth Williamson spoke for the accounting department:

We have over 100 highly dedicated people working in the accounting department, and all of these people approach their responsibilities with the highest degree of integrity. Our corporate philosophy, which has not been crafted in response to all the bad press that accountants have received in recent years, not only encourages, but expects, ethical behavior at all levels of the company. Our focus is to make financial decisions that are in the best interest of our policyholders and employees for the long term.

Pictured above is the 2006 Amica Board of Directors. From left are Robert A. DiMuccio, Jeffrey P. Aiken, Ronald K. Machtley, Cheryl W. Snead, Edward F. DeGraan, Michael D. Jeans, Richard A. Plotkin, Thomas A. Taylor, Barry G. Hittner, Patricia W. Chadwick, Donald J. Reaves, and Andrew M. Erickson.

This corporate culture of customer service and integrity is passed down from Amica generation to generation because, as Dave House of the claims executive department explained, "We are all rooted in the organization, so the culture is passed on and on. ... [Many] people here have 25-plus years of experience."[77]

Henry Woodbridge, a retired member of Amica's Board of Directors, found the Amica culture unique when he first associated with the company back in 1968. "I think that the culture was somewhat unique then, and now I think it is terribly unique," he said. "It is being reinforced, and it is one of the major factors in the success of the company. They have been able to adapt to dramatic changes in technology and competition, and they have been able to do it without losing the basic flavor of the company. I think that is very unique."[78]

According to Stuart Towsey:

The new world is technology-driven. In the old days we could make transitions at a steady, consistent pace. Now Amica is making changes in its processes almost daily, but the core aspects of our business, the adherence to highly moral and ethical standards, remain the foundation of our organization.

Amica has something that is unique. It's a human value that we want to protect and pass on. It makes this company a really nice place to work. It frees you up to do the right thing.

We know that we are in a viable industry, that there will be a need for our products in the future. There is also a need for an insurance company like Amica. The people we've identified as "value-buyers" want a consultative and educational approach to solving their property insurance and liability needs. Our efforts are focused on developing our people and processes to access and service that market. I think the future looks very good for Amica.

Helen MacNeil, her mind on Amica's responsibilities to its policyholders and employees, put it succinctly. "Believe me, it is a humbling thing to have this job, but the company has the best years ahead of it, not behind it," she said.[79]

As Amica reaches its 100th anniversary, President and CEO Robert A. DiMuccio explained: "This company is a special place, and I want to make sure that we move the company forward and prepare for its next 100 years. What very much sets Amica apart is our level of service, which comes from deep within our culture. No one can replicate our service ethic and the long-term tenure of our employees. This creates a sense of loyalty to our policyholders, a loyalty that has been rewarded by their loyalty in return."[80]

Notes to Sources

Chapter One

1. *Pathway of Progress*, Amica publication, 1998, page 9.
2. *A Science Odyssey*, "People And Discoveries: Ford Installs First Moving Assembly Line," PBS Web site, http://www.pbs.org.
3. *Pathway of Progress*, 1998.
4. *Pathway of Progress*, Amica publication, 1957, page 16.
5. *Pathway of Progress*, 1998, 10.
6. A. T. Vigneron letter to policyholders, Spring 1909.
7. *History of Amica*, transcript of company-produced video, 1985.
8. A. T. Vigneron, letter to prospective clients, Spring 1907.
9. *Pathway of Progress*, 1998, 10.
10. A. T. Vigneron, letter to policyholders, 3 February 1908.
11. U-S-History.com Web site, http://www.u-s-history.com.
12. *Pathway of Progress*, 1998, 10.
13. A. T. Vigneron, letter to policyholders, Spring 1908.
14. Letter to F. M. Barber, 20 June 1908.
15. *Pathway of Progress*, 1957, 18.
16. Ibid, 19.
17. Amica company postcard, March 1910.
18. *Pathway of Progress*, 1957, 19.
19. *Pathway of Progress*, 1998, 10.
20. Michael L. Berger, *The Devil Wagon in God's Country: The Automobile and Social Change in Rural America, 1893–1929*, Archon Books, Hamden, CT, 1979, page 13.
21. *Pathway of Progress*, 1957, 19–20.
22. *The Devil Wagon in God's Country*, 51.
23. *A Science Odyssey*.
24. *Pathway of Progress*, 1998, 12.
25. *Pathway of Progress*, 1957, 21.
26. Ibid, 20.
27. Ibid, 21.
28. Ibid.
29. Ibid, 23.
30. Ibid, 22–23.
31. *Pathway of Progress*, 1998, 13.

Chapter Two

1. "The American Experience: Influenza 1918," PBS Web site, http://www.pbs.org.
2. *Pathway of Progress*, Amica publication, 1957, page 24.
3. Ibid.
4. A. T. Vigneron, letter to policyholders, 1924.
5. Amica annual report, 1924.
6. *Pathway of Progress*, 1957, 25.
7. Marjorie Sutton Chace, letter, 1 January 1985.
8. Ibid.
9. Ibid.
10. Ibid.
11. A. T. Vigneron, letter to policyholders, Amica annual report, 1929.
12. "The First Measured Century," PBS Web site, http://www.pbs.org/fmc.
13. 1929 Stock Market Crash Web site, http://www.1929stockmarketcrash.com.
14. Ibid.
15. "The First Measured Century."
16. *Pathway of Progress*, 1957, 27.
17. Ibid.
18. Ibid.
19. Ibid, 27–28.
20. Ibid.
21. Ibid, 28.
22. Ibid.
23. *Pathway of Progress*, 1957, 30.
24. Amica annual report, 1933.
25. Amica annual report, 1934.
26. Ibid.

NOTES TO SOURCES

27. Ibid.
28. Amica annual report, 1937.
29. Lawrence Tingley, interviewed by Amica staff, audio recording.
30. *Pathway of Progress*, 1957, 31.
31. Tingley interview.
32. *Pathway of Progress*, 1957, 31.
33. Ibid.
34. Tingley interview.
35. *Pathway of Progress*, 1957, 31.

Chapter Three

1. *Pathway of Progress*, Amica publication, 1957, page 31.
2. Lawrence Tingley, interviewed by Amica staff, audio recording.
3. Insurance Institute of America, Abel Conference Room dedication ceremony program, 15 June 1979; *Pathway of Progress*, page 32.
4. Gardner Northup, interviewed by Amica staff, audio recording.
5. Insurance Institute of America.
6. *Pathway of Progress*, 32.
7. Amica annual report, 1942.
8. Amica annual report, 1941.
9. Amica annual report, 1942.
10. Amica annual report, 1944.
11. Ibid.
12. Amica annual report, 1945.
13. Amica annual report, 1944.
14. Ibid.
15. Northup interview.
16. Amica annual report, 1943.
17. *Pathway of Progress*, 36.
18. Amica annual report, 1946.
19. *Pathway of Progress*, 36.
20. Amica annual report, 1947.
21. Ibid.
22. Tingley interview.
23. Barbara Smyth, interviewed by Amica staff, audio recording.
24. Don Goodby, interviewed by Amica staff, audio recording.
25. Ibid.
26. Ibid.
27. Phil Lundgren, interviewed by Amica staff, audio recording.
28. Smyth interview.
29. Lundgren interview.

**Chapter Three Sidebar:
Three Decades of Leadership**

1. Amica annual report, 1944.
2. Robert Hanke, interviewed by Amica staff, audio recording.
3. *Amica News*, Summer 1970.
4. *Providence Sunday Journal Business Weekly*, 28 February 1971.
5. *Amica News*, Spring 1977.

**Chapter Three Sidebar:
Women at Work**

1. Susan Damplo, "Federally Sponsored Childcare During World War II: An Idea Before Its Time," Georgetown Law—Published Articles, 1987, http://www.law.georgetown.edu/glh/damplo.htm.
2. "Federally Sponsored Childcare During World War II: An Idea Before Its Time."
3. "Women's Annual Earnings Are Substantially Lower than Those of Men: Statistical Studies on Women Workers," http://historymatters.gmu.edu/d/6471.

Chapter Four

1. David Cassick, interviewed by Amica staff, audio recording.
2. Ibid.
3. Ibid.
4. John Boyce, interviewed by Amica staff, audio recording.
5. Ibid.
6. Harold Hitchen, interviewed by Amica staff, audio recording.
7. Carl Hoyer, interviewed by Amica staff, audio recording.
8. Gardner Northup, interviewed by Amica staff, audio recording.
9. *Pathway of Progress*, Amica publication, 1957.
10. *Amica Newsletter*, June 1950.
11. Ibid.
12. Ibid.
13. *Amica Newsletter*, August 1950.
14. *Amica Newsletter*, November/December 1951.
15. *Amica Newsletter*, January 1952.
16. *Amica Newsletter*, September/October 1952.
17. *Amica Newsletter*, June 1951.
18. *Amica News*, Winter 1953.
19. *Amica News*, Summer 1953.
20. *Amica News*, Fall 1953.
21. Hoyer interview.
22. Priscilla Lowell, interviewed by Amica staff, audio recording.
23. Hitchen interview.
24. Lowell interview.
25. Davies Bissett Jr., interviewed by Amica staff, audio recording.
26. Don Goodby, interviewed by Amica staff, audio recording.
27. Bissett interview.
28. Rodgers Broomhead, interviewed by Jeffrey L. Rodengen, audio recording, 25 August 2004, Write Stuff Enterprises, Inc.
29. Ibid.
30. *Amica News*, Summer 1958.
31. *Pathway of Progress*, 36.
32. Boyce interview.
33. Hitchen interview; Northup interview.
34. Lowell interview.
35. Barbara Smyth, interviewed by Amica staff, audio recording.
36. Philip Lundgren, interviewed by Amica staff, audio recording.
37. *Pathway of Progress*, 37.
38. Lowell interview.
39. *Pathway of Progress*, 37.

40. Hoyer interview.
41. *Pathway of Progress*, 38.
42. Ibid.
43. Broomhead interview.
44. Amica annual report, 1958.
45. Boyce interview.

**Chapter Four Sidebar:
Branching Out**

1. Amica annual report, 1942.
2. *Amica News*, Summer 1958.

**Chapter Four Sidebar:
A Most Important Date**

1. *Pathway of Progress*, Amica publication, 1957.
2. John Boyce, interviewed by Amica staff, audio recording.
3. *Pathway of Progress*, 40–41.

Chapter Five

1. Amica annual report, 1970.
2. Amica annual report, 1964.
3. *Amica News*, Winter 1963.
4. *Amica News*, Summer 1964.
5. *Amica News*, Fall 1966.
6. Andrew Erickson, interviewed by Amica staff, audio recording.
7. Marion Nencka, interviewed by Richard Hubbard, audio recording, 4 March 2004, Write Stuff Enterprises, Inc.
8. *Amica News*, Winter 1963.
9. Ibid.
10. Vince McCullough, interviewed by Jeff Rodengen, audio recording, Write Stuff Enterprises, Inc.
11. *Amica News*, Spring 1967.
12. Peter Goldbecker, interviewed by Jeff Rodengen, audio recording, Write Stuff Enterprises, Inc.
13. McCullough interview.
14. Amica annual report, 1970.
15. Amica annual report, 1967.

16. DeForest Abel Jr., "A Message to Our Members," Amica annual report, 1970.
17. *Amica News*, Summer 1970.
18. *Providence Sunday Journal Business Weekly*, 28 February 1971.
19. "A Message to Our Members."
20. Amica annual report, 1969.
21. Ken Amylon, interviewed by Joe Motta and Michael Walsh, audio recording, 2003.
22. Fred Brown, interviewed by Amica staff, audio recording.
23. Karen Holman, interviewed by Joe Motta, audio recording, 2003.
24. Rich McLaughlin, interviewed by Richard Hubbard, audio recording, 5 March 2004, Write Stuff Enterprises, Inc.
25. "A Message to our Members."
26. *Amica News*, Summer 1967.
27. Amica annual report, 1970.
28. Ibid.
29. *Amica News*, Summer 1970.
30. Ibid.
31. Amica annual report, 1970.

**Chapter Five Sidebar:
Top of the Heap**

1. *Consumer Reports*, April 1962.
2. *Consumer Reports*, July 1977.
3. *Consumer Reports*, September 1984.
4. *Consumer Reports*, August 1985.
5. *Consumer Reports*, October 1988; *Consumer Reports*, September 1989; *Consumer Reports*, August 1992; *Consumer Reports*, October 1993; *Consumer Reports*, October 1995; *Consumer Reports*, January 1999; *Consumer Reports*, September 1999.
6. *Consumer Reports*, September 2004.

Chapter Six

1. Amica annual report, 1972.
2. *Providence Sunday Journal Business Weekly*, 7 January 1973.
3. Amica annual report, 1972.
4. Ibid.
5. Ibid.
6. *Amica News*, Spring 1974.
7. *Amica News*, Spring 1973.
8. *Amica News*, Spring 1976.
9. Ibid.
10. *Amica News*, Spring 1975.
11. *Amica News*, Spring 1976.
12. *Amica News*, Summer 1974.
13. *Amica News*, Summer 1975.
14. *Amica News*, Spring 1976.
15. *Amica News*, Fall/Winter 1976.
16. *Amica News*, Summer 1977.
17. *Amica News*, Spring 1978; Amica annual report, 1977.
18. *Amica News*, Spring 1977.
19. Paul Pyne, interviewed by Richard Hubbard, audio recording, 5 March 2004, Write Stuff Enterprises, Inc.
20. Bruce Maynard, interviewed by Jeffrey L. Rodengen, audio recording, 4 May 2004, Write Stuff Enterprises, Inc.
21. Melburne McLendon, interviewed by Amica staff, audio recording.
22. Ted Murphy, interviewed by Jeffrey L. Rodengen, audio recording, 4 March 2004, Write Stuff Enterprises, Inc.
23. Ibid.
24. Pyne interview.
25. *Amica News*, Spring 1974.
26. *Amica News*, Summer 1976.
27. *Amica News*, Spring 1978.
28. John Boyce, interviewed by Amica staff, audio recording.
29. Donald Goodby, interviewed by Amica staff, audio recording.
30. *Amica News*, Spring 1978.

NOTES TO SOURCES

31. Ibid.
32. Ibid.
33. Ibid.
34. Jim Devine, interviewed by Richard Hubbard, audio recording, 5 March 2004, Write Stuff Enterprises, Inc.
35. Ibid.
36. Lou Peranzi, interviewed by Richard Hubbard, audio recording, 5 March 2004, Write Stuff Enterprises, Inc.
37. Meredith Taylor, interviewed by Jeffrey L. Rodengen, audio recording, 5 May 2004, Write Stuff Enterprises, Inc.
38. Kathleen Curran, interviewed by Jeffrey L. Rodengen, audio recording, 5 March 2004, Write Stuff Enterprises, Inc.
39. John Connors, interviewed by Amica staff, audio recording.
40. Wendy Sturn, interviewed by Amica staff, audio recording.
41. *Amica News*, Fall 1980.
42. *Amica News*, Spring 1983.
43. *Amica News*, Spring 1982.
44. Amica annual report, 1982.
45. *Amica News*, December 1984.

**Chapter Six Sidebar:
Skyscraper Puts Modern
Face on Amica**

1. *Amica News*, Fall/Winter 1976.
2. *Amica News*, Summer 1977.

**Chapter Six Sidebar:
Blizzard's Impact Widespread**

1. Michael Tougias, *The Blizzard of '78*, On Cape Publishers, 2002, page 11.
2. "The Blizzard of '78 Gallery," Massachusetts Office of Coastal Zone Management Web site, http://www.mass.gov/czm/blizzard78.htm.

Chapter Seven

1. Joel Tobey, "A Message from the President," *Amica News*, 1984 Year In Review issue.
2. Amica annual report, 1984.
3. Ibid.
4. Ibid.
5. *Amica News*, 1984 Year in Review.
6. "History Of Amica," company documentation, June 1985.
7. *Amica News*, 1984 Year in Review.
8. David Kenny, interviewed by Jeffrey L. Rodengen, audio recording, 4 May 2004, Write Stuff Enterprises, Inc.
9. Jim Will, interviewed by Jeffrey L. Rodengen, audio recording, 5 March 2004, Write Stuff Enterprises, Inc.
10. Amica annual report, 1985.
11. *Amica News*, April 1986.
12. Ibid.
13. Amica annual report, 1985.
14. Ibid.
15. Ibid.
16. Amica annual report, 1986.
17. Ibid.
18. Amica annual report, 1987.
19. Amica annual report, 1988.
20. Ron Zemke and Dick Schaaf, *The Service Edge: 101 Companies That Profit From Customer Care*, New American Library, New York, 1989, pages 228–229.
21. Stuart Towsey, interviewed by Jeffrey L. Rodengen, audio recording, 4 March 2004, Write Stuff Enterprises, Inc.
22. *Amica News*, August 1985.
23. *Amica News*, December 1985.
24. *Amica News*, February 1986.
25. Amica annual report, 1989.
26. Ibid.
27. Ibid.
28. Ibid.
29. Ibid.
30. Amica annual report, 1991.
31. *Amica News*, October 1991.
32. Ibid.
33. *Amica News*, December 1991.
34. Amica annual report, 1991.
35. *Amica News*, August 1992.
36. *Amica News*, October 1992.
37. *Amica News*, December 1992.
38. Amica annual report, 1992.
39. *Amica News*, December 1992.
40. *Amica News*, April 1993.
41. William DeForge, interviewed by Amica staff, audio recording.
42. Amica annual report, 1992.
43. *Amica News*, August 1995.
44. Amica annual report, 1990.
45. *Amica News*, February 1992.
46. *Amica News*, December 1992.
47. *Amica News*, April 1994.
48. *Amica News*, February 1994.
49. *Amica News*, December 1993.
50. *Amica News*, October 1994.
51. *Amica News*, December 1994.
52. *Amica News*, June 1995.
53. *Amica News*, August 1995.
54. *Amica News*, June 1985.
55. *Amica News*, June 1986.
56. Ibid.
57. *Amica News*, February 1987.
58. *Amica News*, August 1987.
59. Thomas "Bryan" Cook, interviewed by Jeffrey L. Rodengen, audio recording, 5 May 2004, Write Stuff Enterprises, Inc.
60. Kenneth Nails, interviewed by Jeffrey L. Rodengen, audio recording, 5 May 2004, Write Stuff Enterprises, Inc.
61. Bob DiMuccio, interviewed by Jeffrey L. Rodengen, audio recording, 5 March 2004, Write Stuff Enterprises, Inc.
62. *Amica News*, April 1995.
63. Ibid.
64. *Amica News*, December 1994.
65. Dr. Lowell Smith, interviewed by Amica staff, audio recording.

66. Peter Goldbecker, interviewed by Michael Walsh, audio recording, 2003, Write Stuff Enterprises, Inc.
67. *Amica News*, April 1993.

**Chapter Seven Sidebar:
CAT Teams**

1. Amica annual report, 1991.
2. *Amica News*, October 1992.
3. Amica annual report, 1992.

**Chapter Seven Sidebar:
Farewell to 10 Weybosset Street**

1. Amica annual report, 1993.

Chapter Eight

1. Thomas Taylor, interviewed by Jeffrey L. Rodengen, audio recording, 4 May 2004, Write Stuff Enterprises, Inc.
2. Amica annual report, 1994.
3. Ken Amylon, interviewed by Amica staff, audio recording.
4. Amylon interview.
5. Taylor interview.
6. Ibid.
7. Amica annual report, 1997.
8. Ibid.
9. Ibid.
10. Mark Divoll, interviewed by Jeffrey L. Rodengen, audio recording, 4 March 2004, Write Stuff Enterprises, Inc.
11. Francis Maaz, interviewed by Jeffrey L. Rodengen, audio recording, 5 May 2004, Write Stuff Enterprises, Inc.
12. *Amica News*, February 1998.
13. Thomas "Bryan" Cook, interviewed by Jeffrey L. Rodengen, audio recording, 5 May 2004, Write Stuff Enterprises, Inc.
14. Stuart Towsey, interviewed by Jeffrey L. Rodengen, audio recording, 4 March 2004, Write Stuff Enterprises, Inc.
15. Steve Brainard, interviewed by Jeffrey L. Rodengen, audio recording, 30 August 2004, Write Stuff Enterprises, Inc.
16. Stephen Holland, interviewed by Jeffrey L. Rodengen, audio recording, 4 May 2004, Write Stuff Enterprises, Inc.
17. Ron Ranier, interviewed by Richard Hubbard, audio recording, 4 March 2004, Write Stuff Enterprises, Inc.
18. Bruce Maynard, interviewed by Jeffrey L. Rodengen, audio recording, 4 May 2004, Write Stuff Enterprises, Inc.
19. *Amica News*, October 1997.
20. *Amica News*, February 1998.
21. *Amica News*, August 1998.
22. Ibid.
23. Amica annual report, 1998.
24. Bob Benson, interviewed by Jeffrey L. Rodengen, audio recording, 4 March 2004, Write Stuff Enterprises, Inc.
25. Amica annual report, 1999.
26. *Amica News*, April 1997.
27. *Amica News*, April 1998.
28. *Amica News*, April 2002.
29. *Amica News*, April 1997.
30. *Amica News*, June 1998.
31. Amica annual report, 1999.
32. Lee Valentini, interviewed by Jeffrey L. Rodengen, audio recording, 4 May 2004, Write Stuff Enterprises, Inc.
33. Amica annual report, 1999.
34. *Amica Today*, Fall 2000.
35. *Amica News*, February 1999.
36. *Amica News*, October 1999.
37. *Amica News*, October 2000.
38. *Amica Today*, Fall 2001.
39. *Amica News*, April 1997.
40. Amica annual report, 1997.
41. *Amica News*, October 1998.
42. *Amica News*, February 1999.
43. *Amica News*, April 2000.
44. *Amica News*, December 2001.
45. Ibid.
46. Ibid.
47. Amica annual report, 2001.
48. *Amica News*, December 2001.
49. David Kenny, interviewed by Jeffrey L. Rodengen, audio recording, 4 March 2004, Write Stuff Enterprises, Inc.
50. Dennis Giordano, interviewed by Richard Hubbard, audio recording, 4 March 2004, Write Stuff Enterprises, Inc.
51. *Amica Today*, Summer 2003.
52. Peter Cameron, interviewed by Jeffrey L. Rodengen, audio recording, 5 May 2004, Write Stuff Enterprises, Inc.
53. Margaret Munroe, interviewed by Jeffrey L. Rodengen, audio recording, 4 March 2004, Write Stuff Enterprises, Inc.
54. Amica annual report, 2003.
55. "Official Amica Biography of Robert DiMuccio."
56. Robert DiMuccio, interviewed by Jeffrey L. Rodengen, audio recording, 20 June 2005, Write Stuff Enterprises, Inc.
57. DiMuccio interview.
58. Ibid.
59. Ibid.
60. Ibid.
61. Ibid.
62. Helen MacNeil, interviewed by Jeffrey L. Rodengen, audio recording, 20 June 2005, Write Stuff Enterprises, Inc.
63. Ibid.

64. Jim McDermott, interviewed by Jeffrey L. Rodengen, audio recording, 21 June 2005, Write Stuff Enterprises, Inc.
65. DiMuccio interview.
66. Paul Pyne, interviewed by Jeffrey L. Rodengen, audio recording, 21 June 2005, Write Stuff Enterprises, Inc.
67. Ibid.
68. Ibid.
69. Stuart Towsey, interviewed by Jeffrey L. Rodengen, audio recording, 23 June 2005, Write Stuff Enterprises, Inc.
70. Vince Burks, interviewed by Jeffrey L. Rodengen, audio recording, 4 March 2004, Write Stuff Enterprises, Inc.
71. Pat Talin, interviewed by Jeffrey L. Rodengen, audio recording, 4 March 2004, Write Stuff Enterprises, Inc.
72. Divoll interview.
73. Talin interview.
74. Russell Furlong, interviewed by Jeffrey L. Rodengen, audio recording, 5 May 2004, Write Stuff Enterprises, Inc.
75. Tom Buckley, interviewed by Richard Hubbard, audio recording, 4 March 2004, Write Stuff Enterprises, Inc.
76. James Ruegg, interviewed by Jeffrey L. Rodengen, audio recording, 4 May 2004, Write Stuff Enterprises, Inc.
77. Dave House, interviewed by Jeffrey L. Rodengen, audio recording, 4 March 2004, Write Stuff Enterprises, Inc.
78. Henry Woodbridge, interviewed by Amica staff, audio recording.
79. MacNeil interview.
80. DiMuccio interview.

**Chapter Eight Sidebar:
Thomas A. Taylor**

1. Thomas Taylor, interviewed by Jeffrey L. Rodengen, audio recording, 4 May 2004, Write Stuff Enterprises, Inc.

**Chapter Eight Sidebar:
Helping Hurricane Victims**

1. Richard Knabb, Jamie Rhome, and Daniel Brown, "Tropical Cyclone Report: Hurricane Katrina: 23–30 August 2005," National Hurricane Center, 20 December 2005.
2. Eric Blake, Hugh Cobb, Richard Pasch, and David Roberts, "Tropical Cyclone Report: Hurricane Wilma: 15–25 October 2005," National Hurricane Center, 12 January 2006.

INDEX

Page numbers in italics indicate photographs.

A

Abel, DeForest W. Jr., 59, 64, *66,
70*, 71, 74–75, *75*, 76–77,
76, 82, *84*, 85
    Junior Achievement Program
and, 80
    merger of Automobile Mutual
Insurance Company of
America and Factory
Mutual Liability Insurance
Company of America, 73
    retirement of, 85, 87
Abel, DeForest W. Sr., *41*, *48*, *70*,
76, 101
    Amica's 50th anniversary
and, 56
    automobile accidents and, 53
    branch offices and, 49, 50
    business development and,
45, 57
    career of, 35–37, 41, 66–67
    customer service and, 48
    death of, 77–78
    ethics and, 47, 52
    management style, 42, 44
    World War II and, 35, 38, 39
accident reports, 15, *22*, *23*, 32–33
accidents, automobile, *31*
    in the 1940s, 37
    fault and, 23–24
    health insurance and, 57
    increased risk of, 30–31, 53
    liability insurance and, 17
accounting department, 83, 99,
103, 130
activities for employees, 37, 44,
49–50, 65, 79, 80

Adams, Roxanna, *115*
adjusters. *See* claims adjusters
advertising, *36*, *108*, *109*
    1920s and, 25
    21st century, 123
    Amica News and, 71
    marketing letters, 13, *14*
    Robert A. DiMuccio and,
126–27
    strategic planning and, 108–9,
111–12
    Thomas A. Taylor and, 110
agents. *See* soliciting agents
Ahlert, Linda, *115*
Aiken, Jeffrey P., *130*
air conditioning, 64
airplanes, 17
alcohol, availability of, 30
alcohol awareness programs,
119–20
Almond, Lincoln, 100, *103*
A.M. Best Company, 91, 97, 98,
114, 122
American Cancer Society, 119
American Insurance Services Group
(AISG), 124
American Red Cross, 39, 121, 124
Amica
    50th anniversary of, 56, 57
    Amica Life Insurance Company, 70,
77, 90–91, 127. *See also*
offices, of Amica
    Factory Mutual Liability
Insurance Company of
America and, 21, 23–25, 73
    founding of, vi
    motto of, 24–25
    name of, 19, 37

Amica Building, Providence, Rhode
Island
    in the 1940s, 37
    company growth and, 76, 77
    name of, 46
    pictures of, *46*, *47*, *66*, *72*, *77*, *86*
    sale of, 98, 99, 101
Amica Center. *See* Lincoln, Rhode
Island offices
Amica Citizenship Grant Program,
118
Amica Companies Foundation,
118–19, 121
Amica Credit Corporation, 30
Amica Life Insurance Company,
70, 77, 90–91, 120, 123,
127, 130
Amica Mutual Insurance Company.
See Amica
Amica News
    50th anniversary and, 56
    advertisements and, 71
    branch offices and, 49
    on computers, 62, 63
    covers of, *50*, *51*, *67*, *71*, *88*, *91*,
97, *98*, *99*
    DeForest W. Abel Jr. and, 85
    DeForest W. Abel Sr. and, 41,
67, 77–78
    Joel N. Tobey and, 105
    origins of, 48–51
Amica press building, *69*, 70
Amica Savings Plan, 85
Amica Song, 59–60, *60*
Amica Today, 117–18, 123, *126*
Amylon, Ken, 68–69, 107, 108
Anderson, Henry William, *21*, 26,
28–29, 35

INDEX

Anderson, Jack, *79*
annual reports
    of 1964, 65
    of 1968, 67
    covers of, *28, 29, 40, 44, 64, 67*
annual statements, *32*
answering services, 116
application for insurance, *15*
ASPECT telephone system, 127
assigned risk department, 76, 77
automobile industry, 11, 18, 21, 117
automobile insurance, 11, 39, 71, 112
Automobile Mutual Insurance Company of America (Amica). *See* Amica
automobiles
    early models of, 11, 13, *18*
    ownership of, 21, 29–30, 47, 59
    sales of, 18
    technological advances in, 17, 31
    World War II and, 35, 38, 39
auto racing, 17
Shameen Awan and, 125

B

Barber, F. M., 16
Bates, Ron, 68
Bell, Norm, 82
benefits, employee, 44, 57, 71, 85, 114–15
Benson, Bob, 114
Bisignano, Fran, *79*
Bissett, Dave Jr., 52–53
Blair, John W., 44, *76*
Blériot, Louis, 17
Blizzard of 1978, 80, 81, *81*, 82, 101
Blue Cross & Blue Shield of Rhode Island, 115
Board of Directors, *76*, *130*
    DeForest W. Abel, 66, 67
    founding of Amica and, 13, 15
    Joel N. Tobey and, 87, 105
boats
    marine insurance for, 75
bonuses, 26, 56, 57, 114–15
Boston Post, The, 36
Bowler, Jeremy, *106*
bowling leagues, 37, 44, 80
Boyce, John, 42, 47, 48, 54, 56, 57, 80, 82
Boylan, Mr., *58*
Brainard, Steve, 112
branch offices
    Amica News and, 51
    computers and, 63
    customer service and, 31
    expanding nationwide and, 49, 50, 53, 57
    Joel N. Tobey and, 87
    natural disasters and, 92, 93, 94, 125
    newspaper headlines, 60–61
    Raleigh, North Carolina, 70
    San Francisco, California, 45
    senior management and, 108
    Springfield, Massachusetts, 40
    Wellesley, Massachusetts, 75
Broomhead, Rodgers, 53
Brown, Fred, 69
Buckless, Mr., *58*
Buckley, Tom, 129
burglary coverage, 33
Burks, Vince, 128
Burt, George, 42
Butler, Al, 41

C

call centers. *See* National Customer Service Center
Cameron, Peter, 123
Campbell, John W., *76*
carbon copies. *See* copiers
Carter, Jimmy, 80, 81
Cassick, Dave, 47, 48, 82
CAT teams, 92, 94, *94*, 95, 124, 125
Chace, Marjorie Sutton. *See* Sutton, Marjorie
Chadwick, Patricia W., *130*
Chambers, Earl, 103
charitable donations. *See also* community service
    Alfred T. Vigneron and, 27–28
    by American people, 71
    Hurricane Katrina, 124
    September 11 terrorist attacks, 121
childcare, 43
Children's Miracle Network Telethon, 119
Christmas cards, *37, 42*
Christmas parties, *24, 26, 30*, 44, *45, 50*, 59–60, *83*
claim cards, 124–25
claims
    in the 1970s, 74
    21st century, 121–22
    automobile insurance and, 14–15
    Consumer Reports rankings and, 61
    customer service and, 16, 32–33, 79, 91–92
    fault and, 23–24
    homeowner's insurance and, 61
    hurricanes and, 33, 92, 93, 94, 96, 124–25
    natural disasters and, 54–55, 93, 94
    settlement check, *22*
    technological advances and, 127–28
claims adjusters
    on call, 116–17
    CAT teams, 92, 94, *94*, 95, 124, 125
    customer service and, 79–80
    natural disasters and, 54
    Thomas A. Taylor and, 110
claims department, *27*, 32, *89*, 91, 107, 110, *121*
Clark, Gertrude, *76*
Clarke, Cleo N., *76*
collision coverage, 21
communications, 117–18, 127–28
    See also telephones
community service, 65, 80, 118–20, *119*, 121, *123*
commuting time, 101
competition, insurance industry and, 87, 128
complaints, 130
comptometers, 61
computers
    in the 1960s, *58*, 62–63, *62, 63*, 64
    in the 1970s, 82–85
    technological advances in, 100, 102, 122–23
Connors, John, 84
conservation measures
    energy crisis and, 74
    World War II and, 36, 38
consultants, marketing and, 109
Consumer Reports rankings, 59, 61, 77, 91, 99, 107, 118
    customer service and, vi
    Thomas A. Taylor and, 107
Cook, Bryan, 102, 112
Cook, Sandra, *79*
copiers, 61, 62
corporate culture, 47, 52, 59–60, 68–69, 78–80, 88–89, 102–3, 113–14, 123–24
    customer service and, 99
    DeForest W. Abel Sr. and, 67
    employees and, vii, 128–31
    professional standards and, 110
    Robert A. DiMuccio and, 126
corporate information systems department, 82, 83, 100, 102, *116*

correspondence
    customer service and, 61–62
    dictation and, 53
    letters of appreciation, 89
    mailroom and, 60–61
    word processing and, 102
corruption
    Prohibition and, 30
cost of automobiles, 17
costs
    insurance industry and, 64–66
coverage, types of. *See* insurance, types of
Crash of 1929, 27
Cremer, Brian, 125
Crocker, Sewell K., 17
Cuban Missile Crisis, 64
Curran, Kathleen, 84
Curtiss, Glenn, 17
customer service, 26, 31, 65, 77, 89, 115–16, 122
    Alfred T. Vigneron and, vi, 13
    Blizzard of 1978 and, 82
    branch offices and, 49, 55
    CAT teams and, 95
    claims and, 16, 79, 91–92, 121
    communications and, 61–62, 127–28
    company growth and, 33, 87, 91, 112
    corporate culture and, vii, 102–3
    DeForest W. Abel, Sr. and, 41, 48
    the Great Depression and, 28–29
    independent ratings and, 61, 99, 117, 118
    National Customer Service Center, 115–17
    natural disasters and, 93, 96–97
    policyholders and, 23–24, 53, 89–90
    technological advances and, 84–85
    Thomas A. Taylor and, 107
    Web site and, 117
    World War II and, 39

D

Dale, Charles M., 76
Damplo, Susan, 43
data processing department. *See* corporate information systems department
deferments, vi, 38, 41
DeForge, Bill, 96–97

DeGraan, Edward F., *130*
departments
    accounting department, 103, 130
    assigned risk department, 76, 77
    claims department, *89*, 107, 110
    corporate information systems department, 82, 83, 100, 102, *116*
    investment department, 103
    presidents of Amica and, 107, 110
    rating information services department, 84
    strategic planning and, 104–5
    underwriting department, 61–62, 63, 75, 102, 107
Desrosiers, Lori, *115*
Devine, Jim, 82–83
Dewing, Donald, 44
dictation, 53
DiMuccio, Robert A., vii, 103, *106*, 124, 126–27, *128*, *130*, 131
direct mail advertising, 109
disaster preparedness kits, 123
disasters. *See* natural disasters
discounts, on premiums, 64–65
disk drives, 82
diversity ambassadors, *118*, 120, 126
Diversity Works Conference, 120
dividends, 12–13, 15, 17, 18, 21, 65
Divoll, Mark, 111–12, 129
Dolan, Steve, 122
Downey, Jane, 51
dress code, 40–41, 42, 59, 69, 110
Durnin, Jack, *81*

E

earthquakes, 49, 91, 92, 93, 95, 123
Eaton, Ed, 50
economy, U.S.
    in the 1970s, 73–75
    21st century, 120, 122
    the Great Depression and, 27–33
Eisenhower, Dwight D., 505
Emerson, Ralph Waldo, 24–25
Employee Assistance Program (EAP), 115
employees, *20*, *25*, 26, *27*, *30*, 32–33, 37, 47–48, 51–53, *73*, *89*, *93*
    activities for, 37, 44, 49–50, 65, 79, 80
    benefits for, 40, 44, 57, 71, 85, 114–15
    community service by, *119*
    corporate culture and, vii, 59, 128–31

corporate information systems department, 102, *116*
    customer service and, 61, 112, 115–16, 128
    diversity training, 120
    length of service, 88, 128–29
    number of, 60, 75, 83, 85
    offices and, 101
    post-war years and, 40–42
    women as, 69
    World War II and, 35, 38–39, 43
    See also corporate culture
energy crisis, 74
environmental sensitivity, 99–100
Erickson, Andrew M., 61–62, 104, 108–109, *130*
ethics. *See also* corporate culture
    corporate culture and, 68, 79–80, 102–3
    DeForest W. Abel and, 47, 52, 56
    Robert A. DiMuccio and, 126
    Statement of Corporate Mission, 89, 90
    technological advances and, 123
    Thomas A. Taylor and, 114

F

Factory Mutual Liability Insurance Company of America, 17, 18, 19, 21, 23–25, 28, 41, 56, 73, 75
family life, 69
fault, automobile accidents and, 23–24
Field, Richard M., *76*
50th anniversary of Amica, 56, 57
filing systems, 83–84
financial status
    1920s and, 25
    dividends, 12–13, 15, 17, 18, 21
    earnings, 21
    operating expenses, 54
    profitability and, 114
fitness center, 101, *102*
Forces of Nature (film), 123, *127*
Ford, Henry, 11, 17
Ford Motor Company, 17, 18, 21
40 Westminster St., Providence, Rhode Island, *72*, 76, 77, *78*, 97–98
Fratantuono, Sandy, *79*
Furlong, Russ, 129

G

general liability insurance, 33
GI Bill, 47

Gifford, Fred, *81*
Giordano, Dennis, 123
Goff, Robert H., *76*
Goldbecker, Peter, 63, 104
Goodby, Don, 41–42, 53, 55, 68–69, 82
graphics, public image and, 111
Great Depression, the, 27–33
Greater Providence Chamber of Commerce, 115
Grosvenor Building. *See* Amica Building, Providence, Rhode Island
growth, of Amica, 17, 21, 25–26, 33, 37, 45, 57, 60, 70, 85, 90
    50th anniversary and, 56
    80th anniversary and, 88
    advertising and, 108–9, 112
    branch offices and, 49, 53
    customer service and, 87, 91, 112
    founding of Amica and, 15–17
    new offices and, 76, 77, 97–98
    post-war years and, 40, 44–45

H

Habitat for Humanity projects, *119*
hailstorms, 94, 95, 121
handicaps
    Alfred T. Vigneron and, 12
    charitable trust and, 27–28
Hanke, Bob, 67, 92
hats, 69
health insurance, 57, 71
highway system. *See* interstate highway system
Hirst, Jack, 59
Hitchen, Harold, 48, 52, 54, 103
Hittner, Barry G., *130*
Holden, Parker, 50
Holland, Joe, 112
Holland, Steve, 112
Holman, Karen, 69
homeowners insurance, 55, 57, 61, 62, 75, 84, 91, 93–94, 99, 112, 117, 122, 123, 127
Hoover, Herbert, 30
Hospital Trust Tower, 76, 77
House, Dave, 130–31
Hoyer, Carl, 48, 52, 54
Hunt, Bill, 42
Hunt, Russ, 50
Hurricane Andrew, 94, 95, *95*, 96, *96*, 97, *97*, 98, 124–125
Hurricane Bob, 93
Hurricane Carol, 54, *55*
Hurricane Connie, 54
Hurricane Edna, 54

Hurricane Gloria, 92
Hurricane Hazel, 54
Hurricane Hugo, 92–93
Hurricane Katrina, 124–25
Hurricane of 1938, 101
Hurricane Rita, 125
Hurricane Wilma, 125
hurricanes, 39, 92–93, 94, 95, 96, 124–25
Hurricane Wilma, 125

I

IBM 1410 Data Processing System, *58*, 62–63, *62, 63*
IBM 360, 63
ice storms, 93
Identity Fraud Expense Coverage, 123
identity theft, 123
IMAX films, 123
Indianapolis 500, 17
inflation, 64, 65–66
installment buying, automobile ownership and, 29–30
insurance, types of
    21st century, 126–27
    automobile insurance, 11, 39, 71, 112
    burglary coverage, 33
    collision coverage, 21
    general liability insurance, 33
    growth of, 33
    homeowner's insurance, 55, 57, 61, 112, 127
    Identity Fraud Expense Coverage, 123
    liability insurance, 17, 18, 21, 33, 85
    life insurance, 70, 71
    marine insurance, 75
    no-fault insurance, 71
    personal umbrella liability insurance, 85
    preferred risk insurance, 11, 12, 15–16, 18, 108
    property damage insurance, 21, 39
insurance industry, 64–65, 68, 74–75, 76–77, 85
    business ethics and, 102
    competition and, 87, 128
    mergers and, 113, 114
    natural disasters and, 93, 124
    size of companies, 90
insurance regulations, 122
interest rates, 74
Internet. *See* Web sites
interstate highway system, 40, 47, 53, 59
investment department, 103

J

Jackson, H. Nelson, 17
Jamieson, Mr., *58*
Jayne, Bob, 48
J.D. Power and Associates, vi, *106*, 117, 118, 122
Jeans, Michael D., *130*
Jerome, Jaclyn, *115*
Junior Achievement Program, 65, 80

K

Kane, Stephen, *79*
Kast, Frederick, *121*
Kennedy, John F., 64
Kennedy, Robert F., 64
Kenny, David, 88, 123
keypunch operators, *20*
King, Martin Luther, Jr., 64
Klara, Silvana, 117
Koelb, Clayton, 103
Korean War, 48, 51
KPMG consultants, 109

L

Labbadia, Mike, *104*
landscaping, Lincoln, Rhode Island offices, 100, 113
Laura Carr Company, 44
Lebow, Charles, 51
Leonard, Dick, 82
letters. *See* correspondence
Leukemia Society of San Diego, 119
liability insurance, 17, 18, 21, 33, 64, 85
life insurance, 70, 71
lighting fixtures, 64
Lincoln, Rhode Island, offices, 7–99, *99*, 100, *100, 101, 111*
    public image and, 111, 112–13
Lions Clubs, 119
living expenses, claims and, 94, 96, 124–25
Livingstone, Bob, *104*
logos, 113, *113*
losses. *See* claims
Lowell, Priscilla, 52, 54
Lundgren, Phil, 44, 54, 70

M

Machtley, Ronald K., *130*
MacLachlan, Alexander M., 39
MacNeil, Helen, 122, *122*, 127, 131
mailroom, 60–61
mainframe computers, 82
March of Dimes, 119

marine insurance, 75
marketing. *See* advertising
Market Square, Providence, Rhode Island, *16*
"Mass Rush," 53
Mattis, Walter E., *76*
Maynard, Bruce, 78–79, 112
McCulloch, Vin, 63, 64
McDermott, Jim, 127
McGraw–Hill Companies, 117
McLendon, Melburne, 79
McLaughlin, Rich, 69
McWilliams, Peter, 30
medical care, 57
mergers
    of Automobile Mutual Insurance Company and Factory Mutual Liability Insurance Company, 73
    in the insurance industry, 113, 114
Metcalf, Bill, 50, *76*, *84*
Metcalf, Edward P., 13, *13*
Metzger, Brian, 43
military service, of employees
    Joel N. Tobey and, 87
    Korean War and, 48, 49
    World War II and, vi, 35, 38–39, 40, 41
Minerd, Jim, 88
Missouri (ship), 39
Model Ts, 17
motto, of Amica, 24–25, 53
Munroe, Margaret, 123
Murphy, Ted, 79, 125
Murray, Don, 94
mutual companies, vi, 12, 113–14

N

Nails, Ken, 102
name brand recognition. *See* advertising
National Customer Service Center, *115*, 116, 122, 127
National Hurricane Center, 125
natural disasters. *See also* hurricanes
    21st century, 121–22
    Blizzard of 1978, 80, 81, 82
    CAT teams and, 92, 94, *94*, 95, 124, 125
    claims and, 54–55, 91–94, 95, 96–97
    earthquakes, 49, 92, 93
    Forces of Nature (film), 123
    in Providence, Rhode Island, 49
    weather and, 93, 94

"Navigate Your Fate" program, 119–20
Nencka, Marion, 62
newsletters. *See Amica News*; *Amica Today*
newspaper articles
    Providence Sunday Journal Business Weekly, 73, 74–75
    World War II and, *36*, *38*
New York to Paris Automobile Race, 17
no-fault insurance, 71
North Shore Cancer Walk, 119
Northup, Gardiner, 36–37, 39, 48, 54

O

Oakland, California, wildfire, 93–94
offices, of Amica
    40 Westminster St., Providence, Rhode Island, 72, 76, 77, *77*, *78*, 97–98
    Amica press building, *69*, 70
    Blizzard of 1978 and, 82
    branch offices, 40, 45, 49, 53, 70, 108
    expansion of, 76, 77
    Hospital Trust Tower, 75
    Hurricane of 1938 and, 33
    Lincoln, Rhode Island, offices, 97–99, *111*, 112–13
    technological advances in, 64
    See also Amica Building, Providence, Rhode Island
operating expenses, 54
optimism, 71
Oswald, Lee Harvey, 64
overtime, 44, 53

P

Panic of 1907, 15
parties, 40
    See also Christmas parties
Pathway of Progress (1957), 27
Pawtucket (Rhode Island) YMCA, 119
payday, 54
Pearl Harbor, bombing of, 37–38
Pearson, Albert V., 38–39, *38*, 41
pension plans, 40, 71
Peranzi, Lou, 82, 83
personal computers, 84
    See also computers
personal umbrella liability insurance, 85
Phayre, Bob, *80*

Plotkin, Richard A., *130*
policies
    21st century, 126–27
    Amica's first, 14–15
    assessable, 25
    computers and, 63
    filing systems and, 83–84
policyholders. *See also* customer service
    advertising and, 111
    communications with, 15, 117–18
    corporate culture and, 131
    dropping, 61
    employees and, 26, 61
    mutual companies and, 12–13, 114
    natural disasters and, 91, 93, 125
    preferred risk insurance and, 15–16, 108
    punch cards and, 52
    referrals and, 12, 13, 40, 89, 108, 112
    retention of, 89–90
    selectivity in, 21, 23–24, 32
Post, Russell, 30
postage, 60–61
post-war years, 40–45
Potter, Carl, *79*
Power, J.D., III, 117
preferred risk insurance, vi, 11, 12, 15–16, 18, 19, 21, 32, 108
premiums
    assessable policies and, 25
    company growth and, 77, 85
    dividends and, 12, 15
    homeowner's insurance and, 57
    new pricing system, 127
    punch cards and, 52
    refunds of, 36
    rising, 64–65
presidents, of Amica
    Alfred T. Vigneron, 11–12, 17, 18
    DeForest W. Abel Jr., 66, 67–68, 71, 74–75, 76–77, 85
    DeForest W. Abel Sr., 35–37, 41, 49, 52, 56
    Edward P. Metcalf, 13, *13*
    Henry William Anderson, 28–29, 35
    Herbert B. Vigneron, 28
    Joel N. Tobey, 85, 87–88, 93, 97, 101, 103–5
    Robert A. DiMuccio, 124, 126, 131
    Thomas A. Taylor, 103, 107–8, 126

William Henry Anderson, *21*, 28–29, 31–33
pricing system, 21st century, 127
print advertising, 109, 111
print shop, 51, *52*
Prior, Joyce, *115*
profitability, policyholders and, 114
Prohibition, 19, 21, 30
property damage insurance, 21, 39
Providence, Rhode Island, *12*, 33, 49, *66*
Providence Sunday Journal Business Weekly, 73, 74
publications, 51, 70, 109
　See also *Amica News*
public relations. See customer service
punch cards, 52
Pyne, Paul, 78–80, 125, 127–28, *129*

Q

Quarderer, Scott, *106*

R

radio advertising, 109, 111
Rainer, Ron, 112
raises, 26, 27
　See also salaries
rating department, 32
rating information services department, 84
ratings, independent, vi
　21st century, 122
　A.M. Best Company, 91, 97, 114, 122
　Consumer Reports, 59, 61, 77, 91, 99, 107, 118
　J.D. Power and Associates, 117, 118, 122
　Ward's 50 Benchmark Group, 114, 118
rationing, World War II and, 39, 45
Reaves, Donald J., *130*
recession, of the 1970s, 74–75
referrals
　in the 1980s, 89
　advertising and, 13, 108, 112
　customer service and, vi, 16
　post-war years and, 40
　risk and, 12, 13
regional expansion, 109, 112
residential insurance, 33
Rhode Island Federation of Garden Clubs, 99–100
Rice, Bill, 42

risk exposure
　advertising and, 109
　automobile accidents and, 30–31
　preferred risk insurance, 11, 12
　pricing system and, 127
Rison, Clarence H., *76*
Rivers, Doyle & Walsh advertising agency, 109
Roosevelt, Franklin D., 30
rubber, conservation of, 38, 39
Ruegg, Jim, 129–30

S

salaries, 26, 42, 44, 71
　Alfred T. Vigneron and, 16
　for auto workers, 17
　the Great Depression and, 27
　independent ratings and, vi
　payday and, 54
　raises, 26, 27
　women and, 43
sales, of policies, 12, 25, 31
San Francisco branch office, 55
Schaaf, Dick, 91
Schwab, Bill, *102*
Seff, Dylan, 121
September 11 terrorist attacks, 120–21
Service Edge, The (Zemke and Schaaf), 91
size, of Amica, 90, 91
slogans. See motto, of Amica
Smith, Lowell, 104
Smyth, Barbara, 40–41, 44, 54, 59, 60
Snead, Cheryl W., *130*
softball team, *80*
soliciting agents, vi, 12, 25
speeding, 53
Stadnick, Patti, 119–20
Standard & Poor's, 114
stated value, 54
Statement of Corporate Mission, 89, 90, 113
steam engines, 13, 14
stock market, 27, 91, 114
strategic planning, 104–5, 108–9, 113–14
Sturn, Wendy, 84
Success Sharing Plan, 114–15
Sutton, Marjorie, 26, 27, 50
Sweet, Len, 75
Swift, Miriam, *65*

T

Talin, Pat, 129
Tax Reform Act (1986), 91

Taylor, Meredith, 84
Taylor, Thomas A., *103*, *105*, *110*, *130*
　business strategy and, 121–22
　career of, 103, 104, 110
　company growth and, 105
　corporate culture and, 107–8, 120, 123–24
　customer service and, 115–16
　ethics and, 114
　logos and, 113
　retirement of, 126
　strategic planning and, 108–9, 113–14
technological advances
　in the 1950s and 1960s, 61–64
　in the 1970s, 82–85
　in the 1980s, 88
　21st century, 122–23, 127–28
　in automobiles, 17, 31, 31–32
　computers and, 63
　corporate culture and, 131
　corporate information systems department, 100, 102
teenagers, alcohol awareness programs and, 119–20
Teevin, Jim, 94
telegrams, 62
telephones, 61, 62, 84, 85
　National Customer Service Center, 116, 122, 127
television advertising, 109, 111, 112
tenure, of employees, 128–29, 131
10 Weybosset St., Providence, Rhode Island
　See Amica Building, Providence, Rhode Island
Thanksgiving cards, *68*
Thomas, Bob, 42
time cards, 102
Time magazine, 90
Tingley, Larry, 32, 33
Tobey, Joel N., *76*, *87*, *88*, *102*, *105*
　career of, 70, 85
　change and, 87–88
　corporate culture and, 102–3
　Lincoln, Rhode Island, offices and, 98, 101
　natural disasters and, 93, 97
　retirement of, 103–5
　Statement of Corporate Mission, 90
tornadoes, 54
Towsey, Stuart, 91, 112, 128, *129*, 131
trademarks, 37
transition planning, 103–4

U

umbrella policies. *See* personal umbrella liability insurance
underwriting department, 61–62, 63, 75, 102, 107
United Way, 65, 80, 119

V

Valentini, Lee, 116–17
Vance, Al, 51
Victory Dinner, 40
Victory Dinner invitation, *40*
Vigneron, Adolph T., *11*, *14*, 31
    customer service and, 26
    death of, 27–28
    founding of Amica and, vi, 11–13, 56, 101
    growth of Amica and, 15–19, 23
    insurance policy of, 14
    on policyholder selectivity, 21
Vigneron, Herbert B., 13, 14, 26, *26*, 28
voting rights, for women, 19
Vranizan family, 90

W

Waldorf Restaurant, 42
wall calendars, *68*
war bonds, advertisements for, *34*
War Damage Corporation (WDC), vi, 39
Ward's 50 Benchmark Group, 114, 118
weather. *See* natural disasters
weather, punch cards and, 52
Web sites, *115*, 116, 117, 123
Weir, Erin, *115*
Wellesley, Massachusetts, office, 75
wellness programs, 115
Wesolowski, Pat, *118*
What Cheer Mutual Fire Insurance Company, 11, 13
wildfires, 93–94
Wilks, Ernest C., *70*, *75*, *76*, 82
Will, Jim, 88–89
Williamson, Maribeth, *126*, 130
Wilson, Woodrow, 11
women, 21, 69
    post-war years and, 40–41, 48
    right to vote and, 19
    World War II and, 38, 39, 43
Woodbridge, Henry, 131
word processing, 63, 102
work environment, 88
Worksite Health Awards, 115
Worksite Wellness Council of Rhode Island, 115
World War I, 17–18
World War II, vi, 31, 35, *36*, 37–40, 41, 43, 45, 48, 49

Z

Zemke, Ron, 91